ISBN 978-0-282-36041-2
PIBN 10847986

HYTHMIC MOVEMENT

VOL. I.

Development of the Rhythmic and Metric Sense, of the Instinct for Harmonious and Balanced Movements, and of Good Motor Habits.

BY

EMILE JAQUES-DALCROZE.

(PRICE FOUR SHILLINGS AND SIXPENCE.)

1920

LONDON: NOVELLO AND COMPANY, LIMITED.

NEW YORK: THE H. W. GRAY CO., SOLE AGENTS FOR THE U.S.A.

LAUSANNE: JOBIN & CIE.

TABLE OF CONTENTS

PREFACE.

EURHYTHMICS is essentially a matter of personal experience. When asked what it is and to what it leads it is easy for me to explain how I conceived the idea, to quote the actual results, to demonstrate some of the exercises, but the real answer is only to be obtained by actual experience of the Method. A scientist may describe to you the theoretical and practical application of electricity, or of radium, but that does not explain what these two great forces are. You may read all the histories of religion which have ever been written and yet not experience religious faith.

In evolving the educational system of Eurhythmics some twelve years ago I certainly did not realise the great influence that this new system would have in restoring man to knowledge of himself—of this I shall speak later. I thought only of making my pupils better musicians. From the outset of my career as Professor of Harmony at the Geneva Conservatoire I found that for nine-tenths of my pupils harmony was merely a question of mathematics, that they could not hear the chords they wrote down and therefore were unable to appreciate music to the full extent. Music is not purely intellectual; it works through the senses—it sets our whole organism in vibration. If this organism is incapable of responding in all its parts, the brain will register incomplete sensations. At the time of which I am speaking I was thinking more particularly of the sense of hearing, and it seemed to me necessary to train the ears of my pupils, to teach them the practice of the art before embarking on the theoretical side.

The exercises in ear-training which I gave to adults were attended with such success that I determined to make the same experiment with children. I was sure that with them the

It seemed to me that a system in which the muscles are trained to contract and relax rhythmically must result in strengthening the metric and rhythmic instincts; so I invented some exercises in marching, arm-movements, and movements of the body for my little pupils, to be carried out in time to and in accordance with the nuances of the music, and was convinced that this would teach them to become rhythmical. But now my difficulties began. During the first lessons I found that the children, even those most gifted from the physical and intellectual standpoints, did not all respond in the same way. Some responded too slowly, some too quickly to the word of command; some who were able to carry out an exercise with ease in a certain tempo were unable to change to another quickly, however much they wished to do so; others again could begin an exercise perfectly, but were not capable of sustained effort. Judging from my observations, I saw that it was not enough to grasp a rhythm mentally and to have the necessary muscular equipment to carry it out; it was also necessary, in order to insure a good interpretation, to establish a close relation between the thought and the action.

This relation depends on the condition of the nervous system. It is unfortunately rare nowadays for our faculties to be equally balanced, and for mind and body to be in complete harmony. The relation between the faculties which conceive an idea and those which carry it out is often weak owing to the lack of orientation in the nerve impulses, or to a resistance in certain muscles caused by slowness of mental action. It is the consciousness of this continual struggle to make our muscles respond, and of a weakness in our nervous system, which causes mental confusion, lack of confidence in one's own powers, fear of oneself. This general state of uneasiness also results in lack of power of concentration. The brain is a prey to incessant demands which prevent it from working calmly, from carrying out its orders, and from controlling the body with the necessary confidence and deliberation.

The more ordered our life is, the freer we feel. The more words we have in our vocabulary, the richer our thought will be. If we can teach our bodies to work automatically, our minds will have more time and freedom for higher things. If we are obliged always to be thinking of our bodies we must perforce lose some of our liberty of mind. Without doubt the majority of mankind are the slaves of their bodies, prisoners in matter, and, contrary to what is generally believed, the over-cultivation of intellectualism, of analytical studies and of specialized psychology, tends rather to trouble and disturb the mind than to render it lucid and calm.

Many parents and teachers are at pains to prevent children from seeing anything which suggests the classic human form, or from learning anything of the anatomy of the human body which would lead to a liberal appreciation of movement. This has not the desired result of keeping them pure-minded. but inclines rather to the opposite. My pupils have often told me of the horror of some people at hearing that we carry out our exercises with bare feet and legs. These people assert that this is liable to arouse evil thoughts. There is only one answer to such accusations: namely, that to the pure all things are pure, and that if anyone is shocked at the sight of a naked leg it is his unhealthiness of mind which is to be deplored. An acquaintance with the human body will never trouble the minds of children who have been brought up in a healthy and natural way.

PREFACE.

Our system is based on marching, and therefore the muscles of the foot and leg must be accorded as much freedom as possible. No doctor will disagree with this statement, nor, I trust, will anyone who respects the laws of hygiene. Pianists will agree with me that they could not acquire a good technique of their instrument by practising in gloves.

We have two ends in view with our exercises: firstly to create numerous automatic actions and to insure a complete muscular response, and secondly to establish a sure relation between mind and body. One of the first results of these exercises is to teach the child to know and to control himself. Knowing something about the marvellous mechanism of the body—that body which was given us not to be despised but to be made a fit dwelling-place for the soul—knowing also that he is able to carry out with ease movements suggested by others or willed by himself, the child develops the desire to make use of the many forces at his disposal, and as a natural result of his mind being freed from physical restraint, his imagination develops.

Our organs are developed by use; our mental powers are developed by conscious control of the body. As we become freed from physical restraint and from the more elementary forms of mental preoccupation we experience a sense of joy. This joy is a new factor in moral progress, a new stimulant to the will.

All the exercises of Eurhythmics aim at strengthening the power of concentration, at keeping the body under control while awaiting orders from the intellect, at turning conscious action into subconscious, and at deliberately training and developing the subconscious faculties. Further, these exercises tend to create more motive habits, new reflexes, to obtain the greatest result with the least effort, and so to tranquillise the spirit, to strengthen the will, and to establish order and clarity in the organism.

The whole method is based on the principle that theory must follow practice, that rules must not be taught to children until they have themselves experienced the facts that gave rise to the rules, and that the first thing one must teach them is to know themselves. The opinions and conclusions of others should not be taught them until later. Before sowing the seed the ground must be prepared. This is not done either in schools or in conservatoires. As far as music is concerned, tools are put into the hands of the children before they know what to do with them. They are taught the pianoforte before they are musicians, *i.e.*, before they can hear sounds or feel rhythm, before their whole organism is able to vibrate in response to artistic emotions.

The aim of my teaching is to make my pupils able to say at the end of their studies, not "I know" but "I feel," and also to create in them the desire to express themselves; for when an emotion is strongly felt there is an immediate desire to communicate it to others to the best of one's ability. The more life we possess the more we shall be able to spread life around us. To receive, to give, that is the great law of humanity.

I base my whole system on music because music is an important psychic force springing from the emotional and spiritual centres which by its power of stimulation and control is able to influence all our vital activities. It is able more than all the other arts to express the varied nuances of our feelings. Everyone must have music in himself, and by music I mean what the

Greeks meant, *i.e.*, the ensemble of the faculties of our senses and of our spirit, the ever-changing symphony of feelings created spontaneously, transformed by the imagination, regulated by rhythm, harmonized by consciousness. This music constitutes the personality of the individual, and I hold that an education having for its aim the desire to establish intimate relations between the conscious and the sub-conscious, to stimulate and organize our feelings and sensations, must develop our individual character.

I said before that Eurhythmics—on whatever lines it is taught—is more than a pedagogic method. It is indeed a force—analogous to electricity or to the great chemical and physical forces of Nature—which has the power of restoring us to a knowledge of ourselves, of making us aware not only of our own forces but also of those of others—the forces of humanity. It compels us to a knowledge of the unfathomable depths of our ~~enigmatic and~~ ever-changing being; it inspires us with a prescience of the secret of that eternal mystery which has governed the life of mankind throughout the centuries; it gives to our mind a character of primitive religiousness which elevates it and unites in it past, present, and future. And therefore it seems to me that it has the mission of creating in a still far distant future closer relations between body and spirit, of unifying the moral and physical forces of the individual, and of regulating the relations of man to man on a surer basis.

I think no artist who has thought and observed will deny that a conscientious study of rhythm in all its forms tends to a more lively understanding of art. Art is made up equally of imagination, thought, and emotion. Thought tempers and gives style to the imagination. Imagination animates and vivifies style, and emotion ennobles and renders sensitive the products of thought and imagination.

It may be questioned by some whether it is really worth while to familiarise thousands of young people with the structure of art with a view to public performance. But artistic studies have not by any means in view the one and only object of educating artists who can convey to the public æsthetic impressions. They also have the end in view of educating a public which shall be able to appreciate artistic performances, to enter into them, to feel themselves those emotions which others undertake to express.

The instruction given in school is not sufficient. The education of the senses and of the spirit should aim at raising the minds of the general public to such a level that, as M. Adolphe Appia has it, they may themselves become real collaborators in those artistic and symbolic representations which the most gifted people are able to give them. I am convinced that education through and for rhythm is able to awaken the artistic sense in all who go in for it; and that is why I shall fight to the end to have it introduced into schools and to make educationists understand the important and positive rôle which art should play in the education of the people.

It is not enough, as far as the arts of painting, architecture, and sculpture go, to have schools where the representation of line, colour, light and shadow, contrast, and grouping is taught; the pupils of these schools must be taught to feel in themselves the rhythm which arranges, defines, gives balance to, harmonises and animates works of sculpture, architecture, and painting. Nor is it enough to teach the pupils of conservatoires to interpret with their fingers the masterpieces of music; above all they must be initiated into the feelings of the composers, which gave rise to the music, into the movement which had made their feelings immortal, into the rhythm which governs and gives style to the music. A fugue of Bach is a dead thing for those people who do not themselves experience the conflicts of antagonistic elements creating contrast, and the harmony of the co-operating elements which give a feeling of peace and concord.

The ideal teacher must be at the same time psychologist, physiologist, and artist. A perfect citizen on leaving school should be able to live not only normally but also fully. He should be able to create and also to sympathise with the feelings of others. All who train for teachers will not become ideal teachers, nor their pupils perfect human beings; but an enormous effort to this end should be made. An artistic education of which physical exercise forms a large part is the only sure means of soothing our over-excited nerves. If this exercise is taken mainly in the way of sport and games it will overstep the mark and create generations devoid of feeling. It is necessary that in education intellectual and physical development should play an equally important part, and it seems to me that Eurhythmics would have a good influence in both these directions.

E. JAQUES-DALCROZE.

IMPORTANT NOTICE TO THE READER

This book has been written for the use of pupils taking courses in Eurhythmics at the Institut Jaques-Dalcroze and at schools which have acquired the right to teach the Dalcroze Method. Its object is to help pupils to recapitulate and analyse the ideas they have gained in the course of their practical work. Only those who have personal experience of this special form of education can make use of the book, for Eurhythmics is above all a matter of practical experience, and readers who have not had this experience, under the direction of a fully-trained and certificated teacher, cannot claim the right to teach the method. This is especially so since a close relationship exists between the rhythmic exercises and the music by which they are controlled in time and space, and no study of this relationship will be found in this volume. Moreover the reader will find no instructions as to methods of gaining power to improvise at the pianoforte, without which the teaching of Eurhythmics is impossible.

E. JAQUES-DALCROZE.

BIBLIOGRAPHY.

Le Rythme musical. MATHIS-LUSSY (HEUGEL & Co., 2 bis rue Vivienne, Paris).

Musical Expression. MATHIS-LUSSY (NOVELLO).

NOTE ON THE ILLUSTRATIONS.

It is much harder than one thinks to illustrate an educational treatise on bodily movement in such a way as to express not only the actual movements but also their continuity, their initial preparation, their specific end and aim, and the way in which they affect general bodily equilibrium.

I approached many clever artists on the matter, but I had to return their drawings because they were too static in expression and gave no suggestion of movement.

M. Paulet Thévenaz's drawings meet this necessity, and the reason may doubtless be found in the fact that this artist has studied Eurhythmics for a long while and teaches it himself.

Possibly the illustrations in this volume may appear somewhat *æsthetic* for a pedagogical book. But what matter, since they suggest intense vitality and make the explanations of the exercises in the text quite clear, and since also their most striking characteristics are just those qualities of joy and spontaneity which the art of movement claims as essentially its own?

E. J.-D.

EXPLANATIONS AND GENERAL RULES

IMPROVISATION.

Every teacher of Eurhythmics should have made a serious study of improvisation at the pianoforte, and of all the connections between the harmony of sounds and that of movements. He should be able to translate rhythms expressed by movements of the body into musical rhythms, and *vice-versâ*.

TECHNIC OF THE BODY.

As the method of Eurhythmics is based on practical experience, and on the analysis of physical sensations, it is important that the pupil should have a rational training in gymnastics and games. This training should be given in each lesson, or in supplementary lessons. No special system is advocated, but it must be one which aims not only at making the body supple and strong, but also at making the pupil fully conscious of muscular resistances and the laws governing the mechanism of the body. It is the teacher's duty to put the pupil in the way of this knowledge by giving him exercises in bodily technic which will promote suppleness of the arms, legs, trunk, strength in co-ordinated movements, and agility in walking, running, springing on the spot, or forward. *

LINES OF MOVEMENT.

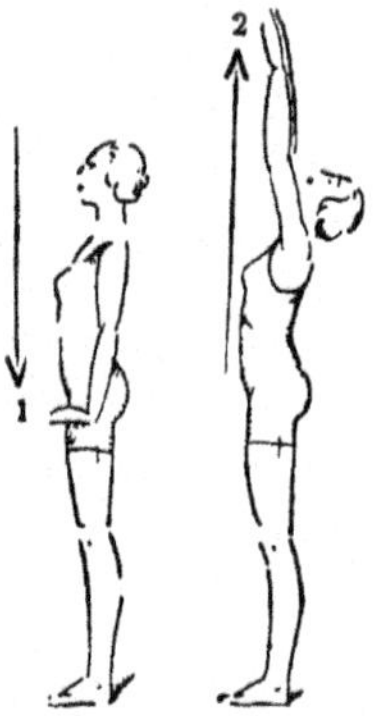

The line of movement from the point in space 1 to the point in space 2 constitutes the first beat. The duration of the sound of the first beat extends from the moment in time at 1 to the moment at 2.

The vertical line ↓ is the strongest; it leads to the moment 1 but belongs to the moment 2 in duple time, and to the moment 3 in triple time, etc., except when it is merely a preparatory movement.

In this connection it should be noted:—

1. That the duration of a beat is limited by two fixed points in space, or by two fixed moments in time.

* See the volume of the Jaques-Dalcroze Method: *La Plastique Animée* (No. 1533, Jobin's Edition, Lausanne. London: Novello & Co., Ltd.).

2.—That both the moment of departure and the moment of arrival can be interpreted in a perceptible or imperceptible way.

3.—That when the moment of departure or arrival is interpreted in an imperceptible way it represents either a first movement after a rest or a last movement before a rest.

The arm which is beating time may pause slightly on the moment of departure or arrival, or at once attack the following movement. This depends on the *tempo*, the extent of the movement, or the force (*see* page 11).

Example.—Here is the beating of four-time with both arms:—

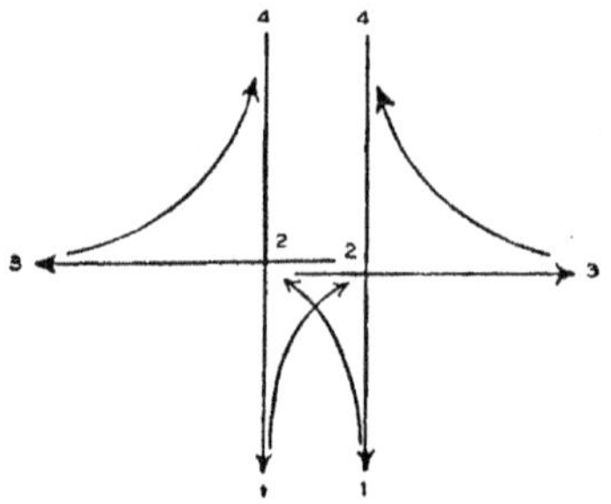

The duration of the *first* beat is determined by the fixed points (moments) 1 and 2:—

The duration of the *second* beat is determined by the fixed points (moments) 2 and 3, etc.

THE DIFFERENT KINDS OF MOVEMENTS.

THE FIVE KINDS OF VERTICAL MOVEMENTS.

The lines of movement denoted throughout the text of this volume are of arbitrary length. To realise their extent the following principle must be thoroughly grasped.

The slower the *tempo* the greater the extent of the movement, and *vice-versâ* :—

1st Kind.—*Wrist.* Upper arm vertical—Forearm horizontal—Movement of the hand only.

2nd Kind.—*Elbow.* Upper arm vertical—Movements of the forearm and hand.

3rd Kind.—*Elbow.* Upper arm horizontal—Movements of the forearm and hand.

4th Kind.—*Shoulder.* Movements of the whole arm from 2 to 8 (*see* the diagram of vertical divisions in space).

5th Kind.—*Shoulder* (from 1 to 9) (Compare page 12 with the five lengths of step).

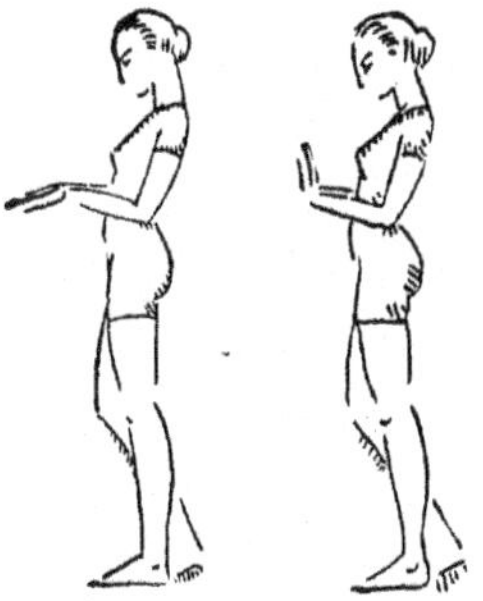

1st kind.

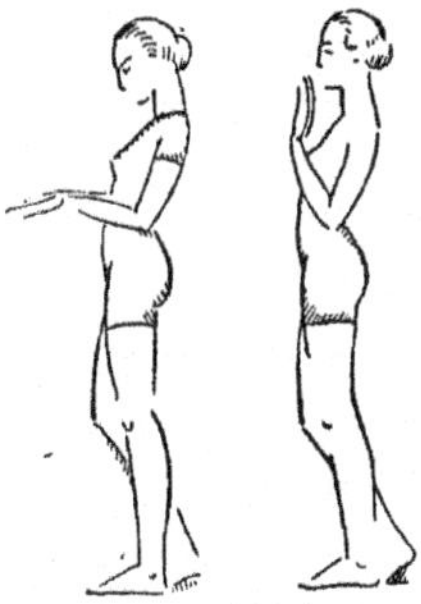

2nd kind.

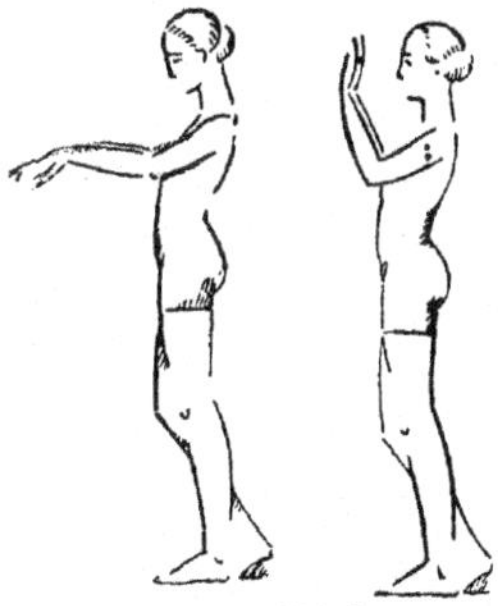

3rd kind.

THE FIVE KINDS OF VERTICAL MOVEMENTS TO BE DONE IN DUPLE-TIME.

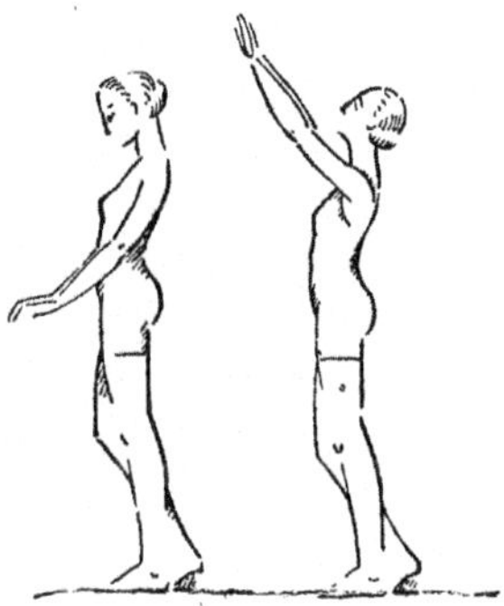

4th kind.

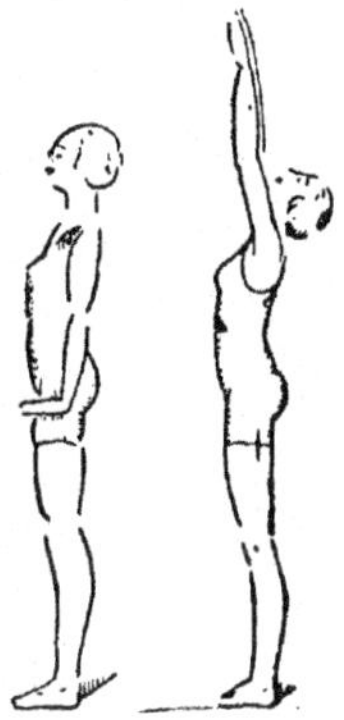

5th kind.

THE EIGHT HORIZONTAL DIRECTIONS.

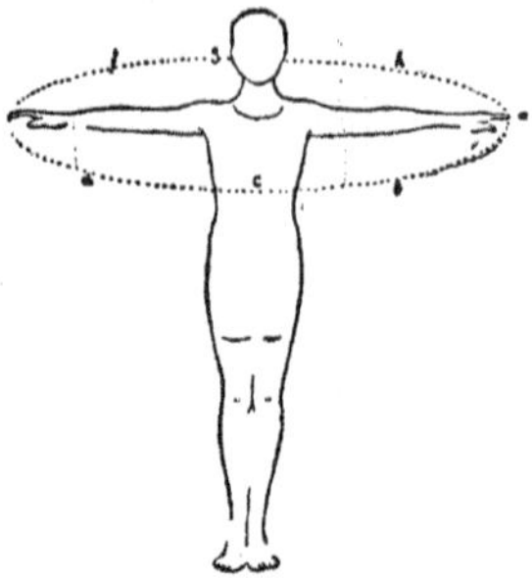

These divide the circular space, in the centre of which stands the human body.

This division is applicable to simple steps, gestures of the arm, springs and lunges.

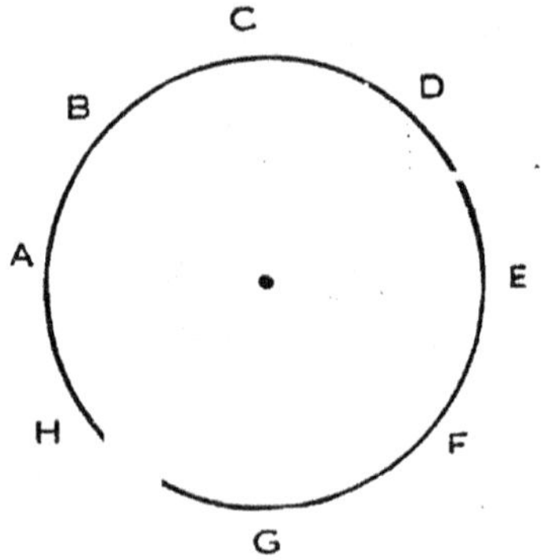

See page 14, the eight directions of steps.

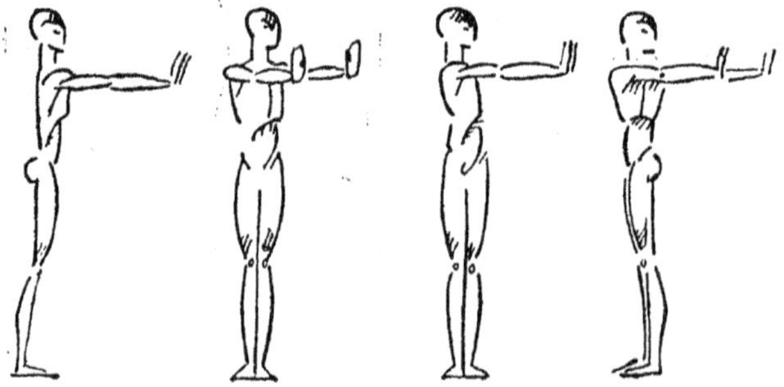

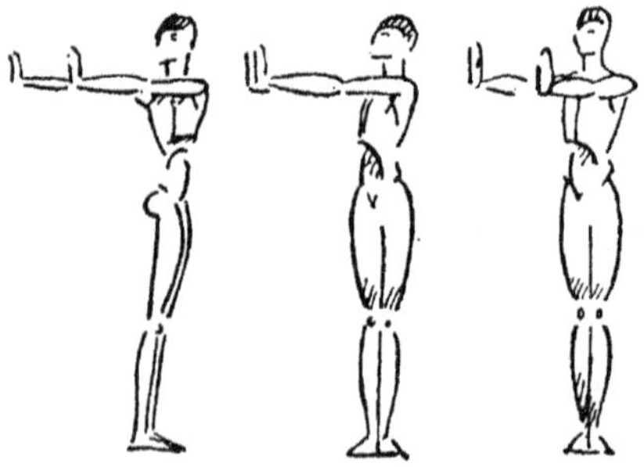

THE NOTE-VALUES OF 2 TO 9 BEATS.

(*See* the detailed study of note-values in each chapter.)

STYLE.

It is the character of the music that enables us to determine which are of greater importance, the points of arrest, of departure and of arrival, or the lines of movement connecting these points.

With the nuances *Legato, Staccato,* and *Tenuto,* we give the chief importance to the points of arrest, and with the nuances *Piano, Forte, Crescendo,* and *Decrescendo,* to the lines of movement (*see* Nuances p. 14).

Tempo is also a component of style, as are all its varieties of acceleration or retardation.

STEPPING.

Explanation of musical signs which specially concern *stepping* :—

(*a*) Each note represents the length of a step, or of a sound.

(c) The moment when another foot begins to move represents the moment of completion of that given sound.

The crotchet (♩) represents the beginning and duration of one sound, the placing of one foot, the beginning and duration of movement of the other foot.

The foot.
The symbol.

The feet.
The symbols.

The first step.—The teacher plays at least two beats in advance in order to enable the pupil to feel tempo.

The last step.—The foot stops moving at the moment of attack of the last sound. While this sound still vibrates, the other foot continues its movement and is placed beside the first one at the exact moment when the sound stops.

A rest lacks movement, but not life.

Tempo.—Notes only represent relative duration. Each of the exercises in this volume should be done in varying tempi.

Accelerando and *Ritardando* only become truly living when they form a perceptible contrast, distinct from the *normal* time.

THE FIVE LENGTHS OF STEP.

We shall call the normal step *Step No. 3.* Step No. 4 will be longer, step No. 5 still longer. Step No. 2 shorter than No. 3, step No. 1 shorter than No. 2. The manner of making these steps will depend on the *quickness* or *slowness* of the *tempo* in which they have to be made, and also on the degree of muscular resistance in the leg. That is to say:—

(*a*) If we want to make a *more rapid* step *with the least muscular resistance* in the leg, when we are walking with the medium step No. 3, we must make a shorter step (No. 2) and the thigh will be raised very little. If we want to walk *still more quickly* with the *least muscular resistance* in the leg, the steps will become *shorter still* and the body will remain vertical, for a short and rapid step does not necessitate a forward displacement of the body. The arms will feel no need of movement either forward or backward.

(*b*) If we want to make a *slower* step with the *greatest muscular resistance* in the leg, when we are walking with the medium step No. 3, we must take a shorter step (No. 2) and the thigh will be raised higher than in step No. 3. If we want to walk *still more slowly* with the *greatest muscular resistance* in the leg, the steps will become *shorter still*, the thigh will be raised as high as possible with strong resistance. The body will remain in a vertical position.

(*c*) If we wish to make a *more rapid* step, *increasing the muscular activity* of the leg, when we are walking with the medium step No. 3, we shall make longer steps, and the body will be inclined forward. If we want to walk *still more quickly* with *increase of muscular force* in the leg, we shall make *still longer* steps, and the weight of the body being thrown well forward will force the legs to run and make springs. The natural swing of the arms forward and backward will become so accentuated (right arm with the left leg) that it will carry forward the body and help the legs to make longer and lighter springs.

(*d*) If we wish to make *slower* steps, with *least muscular resistance* in the leg, when we are walking with the medium step No. 3, we must make *longer* steps with the leg stretched out and with forward displacement of the body.

In a *still slower* time, the leg, kept very free, will be further stretched out, the weight of the body being gradually transferred forward until the toe touches the ground. The arms, slightly contracted, will try to balance the body.

ANALYSIS OF MOVEMENTS IN WALKING.

We shall call the *supporting leg* the leg which has just made the step and now supports the weight of the body, and the *free* leg that which is about to make the movement for a step.

Supporting Leg.—As soon as the foot is placed on the ground, after making a step, the muscles begin to stiffen the joints. This stiffening passes from below upwards.

(4) Hip-joint.
(3) Knee.
(2) Ankle.
(1) Toes, sole of the foot.

Free Leg.—As soon this leg begins the movement for the forward step, quitting the point of departure in the rear of the body, all muscular resistance should be suppressed and

the weight of the body which is inclined forward should carry with it a leg *free* of all weight. While the step is being made, the point of the foot is lowered and the heel raised. First the toes are placed on the ground, then the sole.

The step originates in the hip-joint. The knee, the ankle, and the toes, remain passive.

MOVEMENTS ON ONE SPOT.

The 8 horizontal segments described in the circular space in the midst of which stands the human body. While the body rests on the *supporting* leg, the other leg, the *free* one, can be extended in 8 different directions, quickly or slowly, by steps, without displacement of the body, or by lunges:—

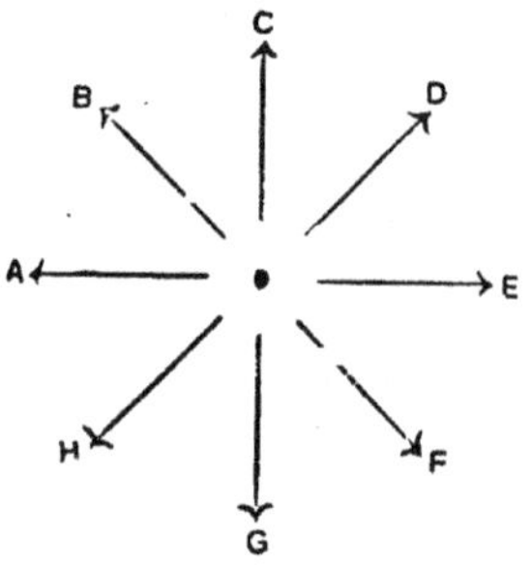

ENERGY.

It would be impossible to conceive of individual will if it were deprived of these three essential factors:—

(1) Imaginative conception of ⎫
(2) Initial willing of ⎬ the act.
(3) Motor realisation of ⎭

The organs of the will are:—

(1) The cerebral cells.
(2) The motor nervous system.
(3) The muscular system.

Hopp.—The order *Hopp* appeals to the centres of control.

Independence of movement is obtained by exercises in contrasting and dissociated movements.

Muscular energy is the result of the power ⎫
Muscular enervation is the result of lack of power ⎭ of the muscles *to contract*, singly or collectively with every degree of *strength* and grade of *quickness or slowness*.

Muscular suppleness is the result of capacity ⎫
Muscular stiffness is the result of incapacity ⎭ of the muscles to decontract with every degree of *strength* and in every grade of *tempo*.

The least effort.—The necessity for *least effort* in order to obtain the realisation of an act is both a [illegible] names are used [illegible]c law. The fact of acting in such a way as to employ the minimum of force necessary proves both that the individual knows himself and also that he knows exactly the act which he wills to perform.

Dynamic gives the life and character of the movement.

An increase of force in a co-operating group causes an acceleration.

A diminution of force in a co-operating group causes a retardation.

An increase of force in a group which is both co-operating and antagonistic causes a *crescendo*, a diminution of force brings about a *diminuendo*.

CARRIAGE OF THE WEIGHT OF THE BODY IN SLOW OR RAPID WALKING.

Slow Walking.—In slow walking (whether forward or backward) the anterior and posterior muscles work together to hold the back erect.

Quick Walking.—In quick walking (whether forward or backward) the upper part of the body leans forward or backward, and the contraction of the muscles of the back is greater in walking forward, the contraction of the muscles of the abdomen is greater in walking backward.

N.B.—It is very important to do the preparatory exercises of Chapters I. and II. (*see* page 23) in every degree of *tempo*.

Note.—The foot (the support of the weight of the body) is sometimes very feeble. In such cases remedial gymnastic exercises are necessary. With weakly children the wearing of sandals with stiff soles frequently causes flat feet. The muscles can be strengthened by accustoming the child to pick up objects with the feet.

Lunging.—The laws of bodily equilibrium show themselves best in lunging. When the muscles of the back relax the body falls forward quite naturally, and the step is the inevitable result of this relaxation. When a vertical position is wanted, following on this lunge, the muscles of the back raise the vertebral column.

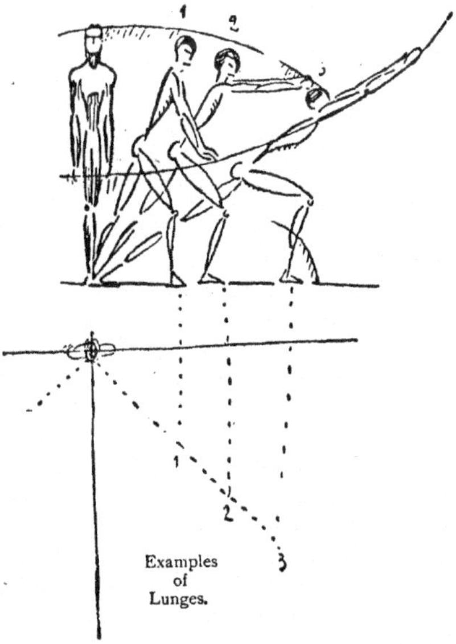

Examples of Lunges.

DIFFERENT MEANS OF PHRASING.

The following are various ways of scanning and punctuating musical phrases:—

(*a*) Entrance of different groups of pupils alternately—

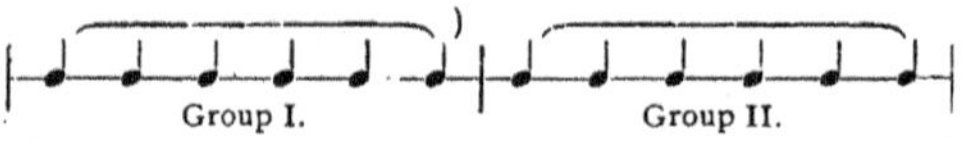

(*b*) Contrasting force—

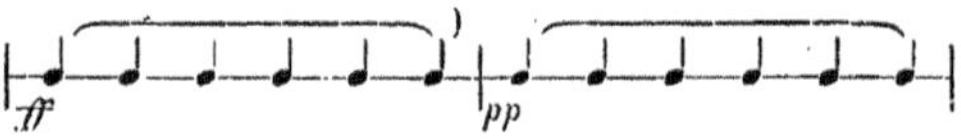

(*c*) Difference in the size of the step (*see* page 7)—

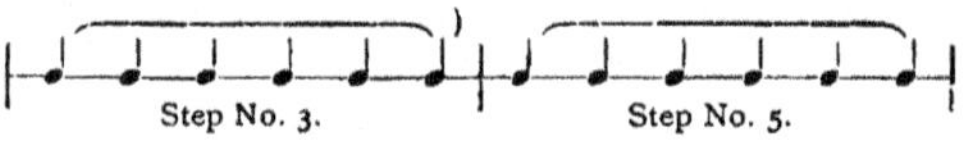

(*d*) Change of direction—

(*e*) Taking up the new phrase with the foot which stepped the last note of the preceding phrase (this necessitates a rapid backward transference of the weight of the body after the break, so as to allow of the raising of the supporting leg which has now become the free one)—

(*f*) Change of the arm beating time;

(*g*) Application of rhythmic breathing—

TABLE OF NOTE-VALUES, THEIR NAMES AND SYMBOLS.

Demisemiquaver $\frac{1}{32}$	Qnaver $\frac{1}{8}$	Minim $\frac{1}{2}$
Semiquaver $\frac{1}{16}$	Crotchet $\frac{1}{4}$	Semibreve 1

The same names are used in 6/8, 3/4, etc.

The notes followed by a dot are called *dotted notes.*

The note twice as long as the semibreve, named a breve, is made thus: 𝅜

GROUPING OF NOTES.

The metrical accent determines the position of the signs for the grouping of notes.

The *bar line* is placed before the chief metrical accent | ♩ | 𝅗𝅥 etc.

The *dotted line.* When the value of the beat is greater than ♩ the *secondary accentuations* may be shown by dotted vertical lines :—

but only in cases where confusion might arise. In values shorter than the ♪ groups of notes are joined by a horizontal line. The first note of each group is more or less accented :—

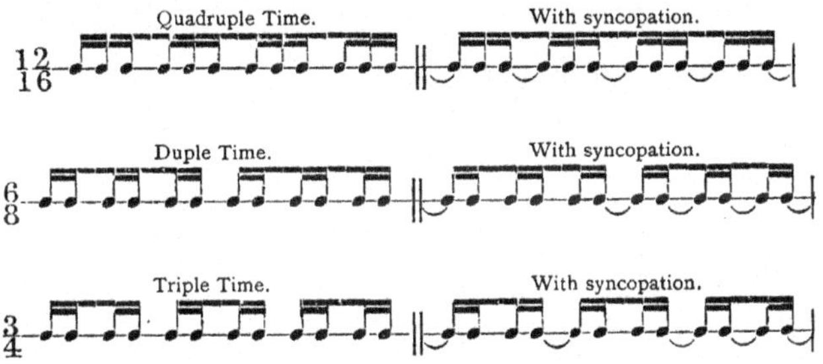

When realising syncopated notes, the length of time taken in bending the knee is regulated according to the moment of attack of the second note of the group (*see* syncopations, page 26).

EXCEPTIONAL GROUPINGS.

When a beat, usually divided into 2, 4, 8 parts, is divided into 3, 5, or 7, as an exception, the following signs are used, 3, 5, 7.

Example :  etc.

And likewise when a beat is usually divided into 3, 5, or 9, every exceptional division is shown by the signs  etc.

Example:  etc.

DOTTED NOTES.

(*a*) Prolongation of a note for half its value:—

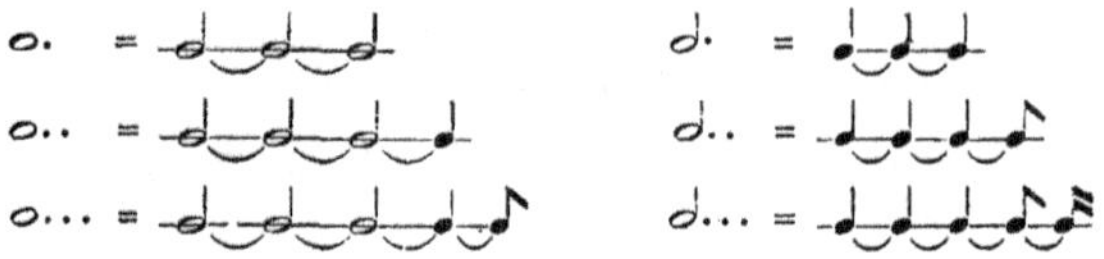

(a dot after the note).

(a second dot after the first).

(a third dot after the second).

(*b*) Prolongation of a note for $\frac{1}{4}$ of its value:—

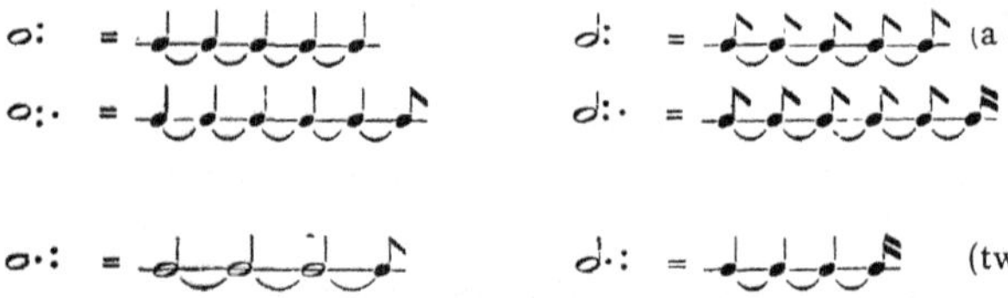

(a second dot under the first).

(a dot after the two dots which are one over the other.)

(two dots one over the other after the first).

(*c*) Prolongation of a note for $\frac{1}{8}$ of its value:—

 (three dots one over the other).

(*d*)

The symbol for $\frac{1}{4}$ of a semibreve is	𝅘𝅥	The symbol for $\frac{1}{8}$ of a semibreve is	𝅘𝅥𝅮
" " $\frac{2}{4}$ " "	𝅗𝅥	" " $\frac{2}{8}$ " "	𝅘𝅥
" " $\frac{3}{4}$ " "	𝅗𝅥.	" " 3 " "	𝅘𝅥.
" " $\frac{4}{4}$ " "	𝅝	" " $\frac{4}{8}$ " "	𝅗𝅥
" " $\frac{5}{4}$ " "	𝅝:	" " $\frac{5}{8}$ " "	𝅗𝅥:
" " $\frac{6}{4}$ " "	𝅝.	" " 6 " "	𝅗𝅥.
" " $\frac{7}{4}$ " "	𝅝..	" " $\frac{7}{8}$ " "	𝅗𝅥:
" " $\frac{8}{4}$ " "	𝅜	" " 8 " "	𝅝
" " $\frac{9}{4}$ " "	𝅜⁝	" " $\frac{9}{8}$ " "	𝅝⁝
" " $\frac{10}{4}$ " "	𝅜:	" " $\frac{10}{8}$ " "	𝅝:
" " $\frac{11}{4}$ " "	𝅜:·	" " $\frac{11}{8}$ " "	𝅝:·
" " $\frac{12}{4}$ " "	𝅜·	" " 12 " "	𝅝·
" " $\frac{13}{4}$ " "	𝅜·:	" " 13 " "	𝅝·: etc.

SIGNS TO INDICATE BREATHING.

1.—[Sudden contraction of the abdominal muscles.

] Sudden decontraction of the abdominal muscles.

Preparatory exercises for ⌐. From lying down rise to a sitting position, *i.e.*, maintaining the abdominal contraction even after it is no longer necessary.

2. ꞓ Sudden expansion of the ribs.

ʒ Sudden contraction of the ribs.

Preparatory exercise for ꞓ. Place the hands on the ribs on each side and resist the expansion of the cavity of the thorax.

3. ⌒ Sudden drawing in of the abdominal muscles, which results ⌣ in the expansion of the ribs and consequent raising of the chest.

4. ⌒ Sudden release of the abdominal muscles.

⌣ Sudden fall of the breastbone and upper chest.

EXERCISES FOR DEVELOPING THE MUSCLES OF THE CHEST.

The following is another preparatory exercise for developing the muscles of the chest:—

Place the left hand on the lower ribs of the right side and expand them with resistance; then cross the right arm completely over the chest:—

(*a*) on a level with the lower ribs,

(*b*) on a level with the upper ribs,

(*c*) on a level with the chin.

The preparatory exercises are to be done *w thout the help of breathing*. Before doing them it is important:—

I. To have a moderate quantity of air in the lungs,

II. Not to have the vocal cords tightened (as in the preparation for the shock of the glottis). In other words, the neck must be perfectly free.

(Light and incomplete inspiration.

< Short but complete inspiration.

<— Slow and complete inspiration.

(Slow and incomplete inspiration.

) Light and incomplete expiration.

> Short but complete expiration.

—> Slow and complete expiration.

) Slow and incomplete expiration.

BREATHING may be:—

A. Diaphragmatic breathing: The abdomen is contracted; the lowering of the diaphragm presses the abdominal organs inward.

B. Intercostal breathing: The cavity of the thorax is enlarged on both sides.

C. Supercostal breathing: The upper portion of the chest is dilated.

These different ways can be combined according to the actions which the breathing is assisting (*e.g.*, singing, manual work), and in the art of *moving plastic*, according to the gestures of one or the other limbs :—

1st	2nd	3rd	4th	5th	6th
A	B	C	A	B	A
			B	C	C

Complete breathing, necessary in rhythmic movement, when no specific artistic nuances are to be expressed, combines the three preceding types:—

A
B
C

Fatigue.—Breathing exercises must never be practised when the pupil is out of breath. They must be carefully done, without too frequent repetition and without exaggeration. In case of dizziness they should be practised sitting down.

See the volume of the Jaques-Dalcroze Method called *La Respiration et l'Innervation* (planches anatomiques Nos. 11, 13 et 15, 17 et 19. No 981, Edition Jobin et Cie.).

N.B.—From the very first lesson the pupil should be taught to write down the rhythms he has realised. Moreover the pupil should be encouraged to compose and write down rhythms at home, in preparation for the next lesson. During the lesson itself the rhythms should be written on the blackboard.

REALISATION—HEARING.

The teacher should insist on complete bodily relaxation while the pupil is listening to the rhythm he has to realise, and on absolute calm and tranquillity of mind while he realises it.

N.B.—The word *hopp* is used as a signal to make a change previously agreed upon.

RHYTHMIC MOVEMENT

RULES AND EXERCISES.

CHAPTER I.

DUPLE TIME.

(The teacher improvises at the piano.)

EXERCISES IN WALKING WITHOUT BEATING TIME.

Preparatory position.—The upper part of the body and the supporting leg form a vertical line. The supporting leg is midway between the points of departure and arrival of the free leg—chin drawn in without exaggeration, shoulders lowered, back hollowed without exaggeration of the lumbar curve, arms hanging naturally. The free leg is placed in the rear at a distance equal to step No. 3.

See page 15: *Carriage of the weight of the body.*

FIRST PREPARATORY EXERCISE.

Swing the free leg forwards and backwards, without any contraction, with a pendulum-like movement. Keep the ribs raised and the thorax open by the help of the abdominal muscles.

SECOND PREPARATORY EXERCISE.

(a) Place the free leg in front, first on the toe then on the heel; bring the weight of the body forward, transferring it on to the leg which has now become the supporting one. The other leg now becomes the free one.

(b) The same backward.

THIRD PREPARATORY EXERCISE.

The same exercise as the preceding one, but the thigh of the free leg is raised in front until it is horizontal, before being placed on the ground. This is a preparation for the stamp.

Important observation: The three exercises should be done in all degrees of tempo.

THE BAR IN DUPLE TIME.

$\frac{2}{4}$ can constitute a crusic or anacrusic bar, *i.e.*, begin with a strong or with a weak beat and be interpreted by a heavy accented step followed by a light one, or by a light step followed by a heavy one.

1. Crusie bar $\frac{2}{4}$
2. Anacrusic bar $\frac{2}{4}$

On the first beat the foot strikes the ground vigorously.

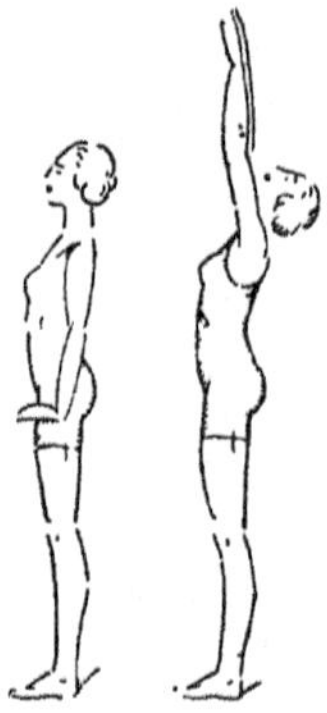

Beat 1. Beat 2.

EXERCISE IN WALKING WHILE BEATING TIME.

Preparatory Exercise.

(*a*) Raise the arm, allowing the hand to hang loosely, then lower the arm, the hand extended, palm to the ground. Close the h ind and stiffen the arm during the time needed for accentuation of the beat.

(*b*) The same with two arms.

(*c*) The same alternately.

(*d*) The same, combined with the preceding preparatory exercises in walking.

See page 7: *Lines of movement.*

PHRASING AND RESTS.

▬ Minim (𝅗𝅥) rest.

⌙ Crotchet (♩) rest.

|⊢ ⊣| Sign of repetition.

) Sign for the cæsura (the end of one phrase, the beginning of another).

PHRASING WITH THE ARMS.

1. Left arm
   Right arm
2. Left arm
   Right arm

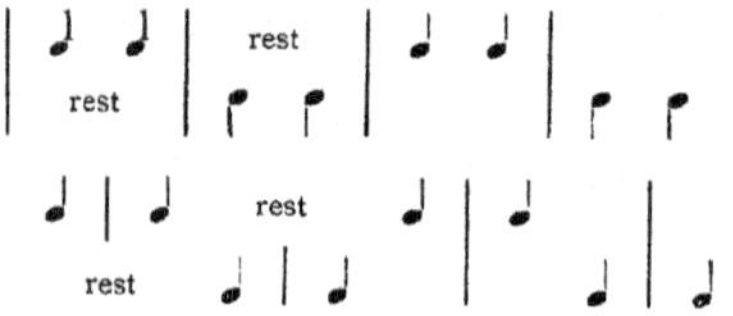

In Exercise 1, the arm is held in Position 2 during the rest.

In Exercise 2, the arm is held in Position 1 during the rest (*see* fig. above).

3. Left arm
   Right arm

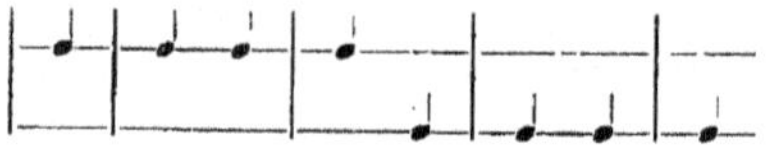

etc.

4. Instead of alternating, both arms make the rest on the same beat:—

(*a*) Left arm and right arm 

(*b*) 

Note.—A rhythm can be longer than a bar:—

5. 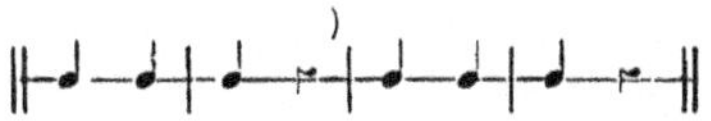

6. 

During a rest breathing can be controlled rhythmically, *e.g.*:—

7. 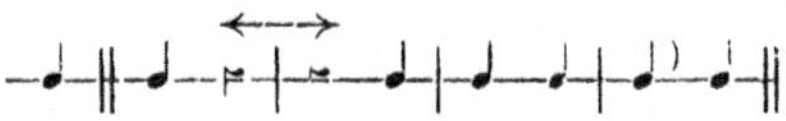

See page 18: *Signs for breathing.*

PHRASING WITH THE FEET.

8. Three bars forward, then one backward  etc.

9. One bar forward, then three backward  etc

More difficult exercises to be taken later: The new phrase is begun by the foot which ended the preceding phrase, necessitating a sudden transference of the weight of the body backward, to make the free leg the supporting one.

10. 

PHRASING WITH ARMS AND FEET.

Exercises 8, 9, and 10 are to be combined with phrasing with the arms.

ANALYSIS OF NOTE-VALUES.

DOUBLE- AND HALF-VALUES.

The Minim 𝅗𝅥 *and Minim by Syncopation* 

Execution: On beat 1, step; on beat 2, bend the supporting leg. The free leg remains free and makes the next step.

There are two kinds of minims:—

(1.) The minim when the step is more accentuated than the bend

(2.) The minim formed by syncopation when the bend is more accentuated than the step

The arm beats $\frac{2}{4}$

Note.—Plastically is easier than ; musically is easier than

1.  2. 

These exercises are to be combined with phrasing. (*See* page 16: *Means of Phrasing.*

QUAVERS.

Execution.—Two equal steps are made to one movement of the arm.

Arms.  Feet. 

A crusie bar made of quavers has only one form.

An anacrusic bar made of quavers has three:—

a.  *b.* 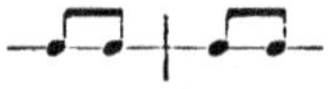 *c.* 

In (*a*) and in (*c*) the arms beat first, then the step follows.

COMBINATIONS OF , , AND

1. 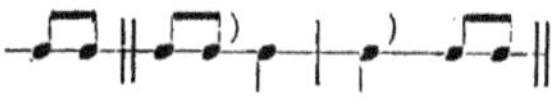 3. 

2. 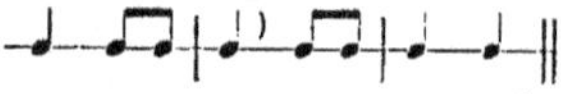 4. 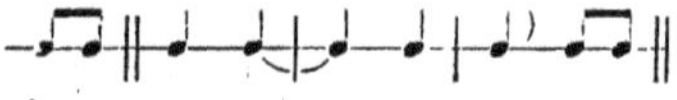

5. 

CROTCHETS BY SYNCOPATION

Execution.—The bend and arm-movements coincide, the step being made between these movements.

Note.—Syncopation is produced either by *retardation* (the entrance of the step delayed) or by *anticipation* (the entrance of the step anticipated).

a. Syncopation by retardation: 

b. Syncopation by anticipation: 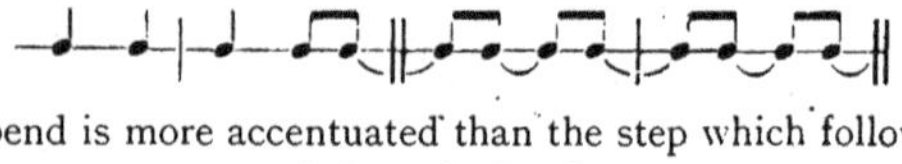

In syncopation by retardation the bend is more accentuated than the step which follows; in syncopation by anticipation the step is more accentuated than the bend.

TWICE AS FAST AND TWICE AS SLOW.

A bar of $\frac{2}{4}$ becomes when taken twice as slow, a bar of $\frac{2}{2}$ | 𝅗𝅥 𝅗𝅥 | A bar of $\frac{2}{4}$ becomes when taken twice as fast a bar of $\frac{2}{8}$ | ♫ |

NOTE.—In this kind of exercise use should be made of the different lengths of step and movements of the arm described on pages 9 and 12.

In $\frac{2}{2}$ the arm beats one beat only for each 𝅗𝅥, and this 𝅗𝅥 is not to be divided in two by a bend. Syncopation when it occurs in this time is still to be interpreted by a bend.

Exercise: 1. Four bars

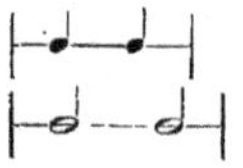

then four bars

Exercise: 2. Three bars

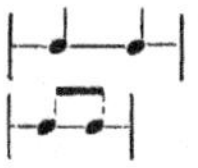

then three bars

Exercise: 3. Two bars

" "

" "

" "

etc.

Exercise: 4. Exercises 1, 2, and 3, making two steps for every arm gesture.

5. *Syncopations* in a succession of four bars of $\frac{2}{8}$, then four bars of $\frac{2}{4}$, then four bars of $\frac{2}{2}$.

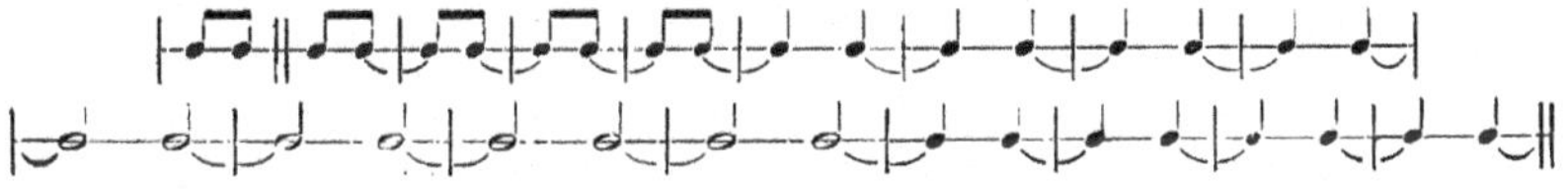

BREATHING.

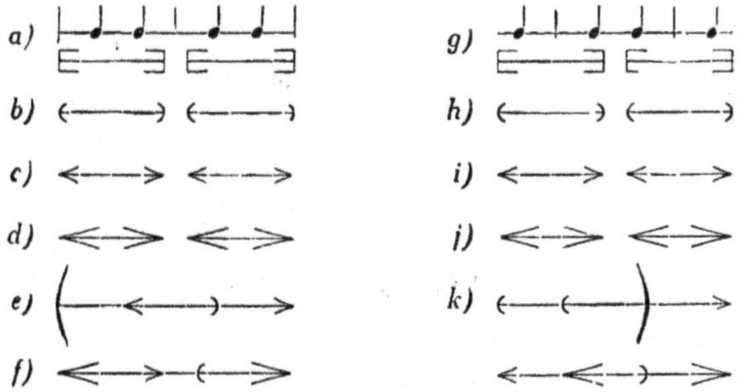

The same exercises are to be done in the position 

See page 18, *Signs for Breathing.*

INDEPENDENCE OF THE LIMBS.

In the following exercises each movement lasts for a ♩ and each complete circular movement has the value of a whole bar.

The exercises are done with two limbs, *e.g.*, with two arms—one arm and one leg—one hand and one foot—the head and one arm, etc.

Independence of limbs—(*a*) one limb *f*, one limb *p*; (*b*) one limb with restricted movements; one limb with extended movements.

EXERCISES IN THE SAME DIRECTION.

1. Two limbs $\downarrow_1 \uparrow^2$ 2. Two limbs $\underset{1\leftarrow}{\rightarrow 2}$

3. Two limbs 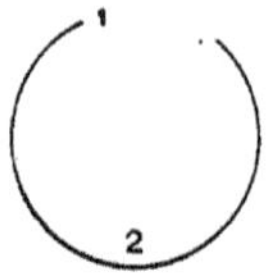 *or* 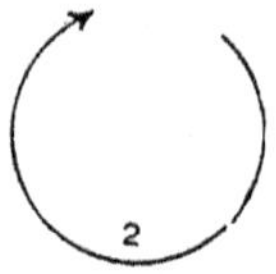

The movements are very simple. Raising and lowering the arms, the thighs, the feet, the hands, etc., then describing circles, passing through the points of departure and arrival $\downarrow_1$ and $\uparrow^2$

MOVEMENTS IN CONTRARY DIRECTION.

4. One limb $\downarrow_1 \uparrow^2$ The other $\uparrow^1 \downarrow_2$

5. One limb $\rightarrow 1 \quad 2 \leftarrow$ The other $1 \leftarrow \quad \rightarrow 2$

6. One limb 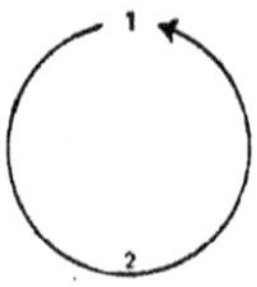   The other 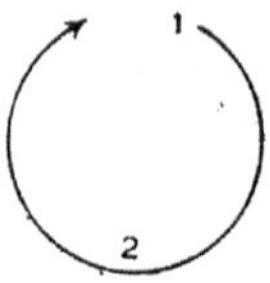

7. One limb $\downarrow_1 \uparrow^2$ The other $\underset{1\leftarrow}{\rightarrow 2}$

LINES AND CURVES.

8. One limb $\downarrow_1 \uparrow^2$ The other 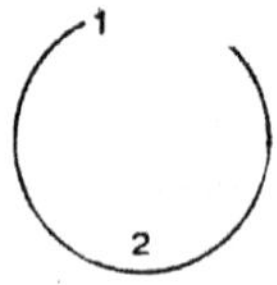 *or* 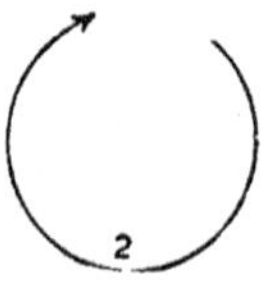

9. One limb ←→ The other 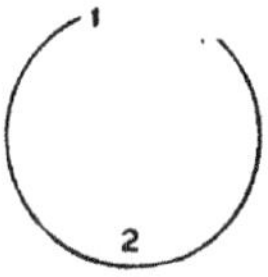 or 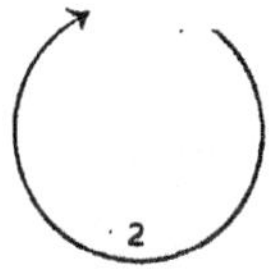

The curve can be horizontal, vertical, oblique, etc.

All these exercises should also be done with sudden changes of direction, controlled by the *hopps* of the teacher, *e.g.* :—

One limb ↓₁ ↑² at *hopp* ↑¹ ↓₂ The other ↑¹ ↓₂ at *hopp* ↑¹ ↓₂

(*see* the following chapter).

EXERCISES FOR DEVELOPING CONTROL AND INHIBITION.

1. The pupil walks | ♩ ♩ | forward. The teacher calls *hopp*, and the pupil walks | ♩ ♩ | ard, then at the next *hopp*, forward again.

2. At *hopp* the pupil walking | ♩ ♩ | interprets the two crotchets by two springs on the foot.
step,

3. One arm beats the bar | ♩ ♩ | A pupil calls *hopp*, and the other arm begins to beat /nile the first arm stops.

4. Exercises 1 and 3 are performed simultaneously.

5. At *hopp* the pupil keeps still for one or more bars, ceasing to beat time.

6. Two ways of phrasing are agreed on beforehand. At *hopp* the pupil changes from one to the other, *e.g.* :—

7. At *hopp* a 𝅗𝅥 instead of | ♩ ♩ | and *vice versâ*.

8. At *hopp* ♩|♩ instead of ♩ | |

9. The pupil walks ♩ ♩ | ♩ ♩ | At *hopp* he makes a spring forward.

10. At *hopp* the pupil kneels suddenly, then gets up at the next *hopp*, etc., etc.

All exercises for independence of the limbs can be treated as exercises for developing control and inhibition, by using *hopp* to indicate changes.

EXERCISES IN HEARING.

1. The teacher plays bars | ♩ ♩ or | 𝅗𝅥 or ♩ | ♩ or ♩|♩ etc. The pupil steps them, and must follow all the *accelerandos*, *ritenutos*, *crescendos*, *diminuendos*, *staccatos*, and *legatos* of the teacher's playing.

2. The teacher plays a rhythm twice, then the pupil realises it. He stands still while the teacher plays a new rhythm.

1.  2. 

. The different ways of phrasing should not be forgotten (*see* page 18). The pupils can form two circles one within the other. The inner one realises the rhythm, then stops, and the outer one in turn realises the rhythm.

3. The teacher plays three 𝅗𝅥's. At the fourth 𝅗𝅥 the pupils walk| ♩ ♩ |

4. The teacher plays ♩'s. At the fourth ♩ the pupils walk 𝅗𝅥's or ♩|♩'s.

5. The pupils are grouped in the middle of the hall with arms raised, and *ring bells*, following the *accelerando* and *rallentando* of the teacher.

6. Pupils grouped in the middle of the hall spring up and down on one spot, following the *tempo* of the teacher's playing. In quick *tempo* little springs; in slow *tempo* high springs with preparatory low bending.

IMPROVISATION.

The teacher asks a pupil to improvise:—

1. Three bars divided into two phrases, separated from one another by a cæsura or break.
2. Four bars, one of which consists of a minim rest (▬).
3. Any sequence of movements alternating with walking, breathing, or conducting with the arms.
4. A sequence made up of 𝅗𝅥 ♩ ♪♪ or ♩|♩ etc.

After one pupil has improvised, the whole class repeats.

EXERCISES IN CONDUCTING.

A pupil stands in the centre of a circle of pupils and beats time:—

1. *Accelerando* and *ritardando*.
2. *Crescendo* and *diminuendo*.

The pupils walk in a circle, following the nuances.

N.B.—The pupils should write down in their books or on the blackboard the rhythms studied during the lesson.

Important Note.—The teacher should often vary the *tempo* in order to accustom the pupils to follow the music, but his rubatos should be logical, and the general character of the time should be clearly indicated.

See: 1. *Marches rythmiques* Nos. 1 and 2 (Lausanne: Jobin & Co., No. 780. London: Novello & Co., Ltd.). *Studies Nos. 1 and 2.*
2. *Esquisses rythmiques pour piano* (Lausanne: Jobin & Co., No. 1528. London: Novello & Co., Ltd.).

CHAPTER II.

TRIPLE TIME.

EXERCISES IN WALKING (WITHOUT BEATING TIME).

Preparatory Exercises.

In triple time the feet stamp alternately:—

1. 

2. 

3. 

During the rests the teacher continues to play crotchets.

4, 5, 6. Repeat Exercises 1, 2 and 3, the teacher occasionally calling *hopp* after the third step, when the pupil should walk three steps more, either forward or backward:—

e.g. 

7. Step all the notes in the bar in $\frac{3}{4}$ time.

ERCISES IN WALKING WHILE BEATING TIME.

Preparatory Exercises.

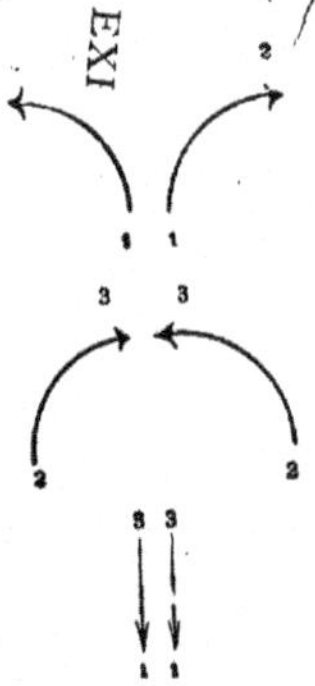

From beat 1 to beat 2, raise the arms sideways to a horizontal position on a level with the shoulders, with a loose wrist.

From 2 to 3: raise the arms vertically, the hands stretched upward, the head following the movement of the arms.

When the pupil is beating time *with one arm only (the left for instance), the head should be slightly inclined towards the opposite shoulder.*

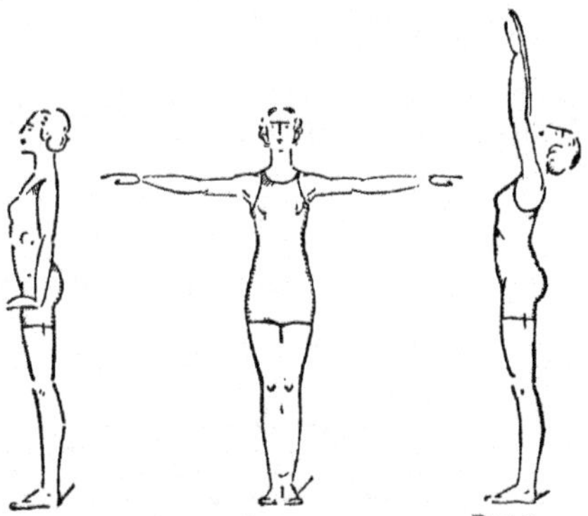

Beat 1. Beat 2. Beat 3.

From 3 to 1, lower the arms; (*a*) with both arms; (*b*) with one arm; (*c*) gestures with the foregoing exercises in walking.

PHRASES AND RESTS.

PHRASING WITH THE ARMS.

1. Right arm
Left arm

2. Left arm
Right arm

THE DOTTED MINIM REST

3. Left arm
Right arm

Combinations :—

4. Left arm
Right arm

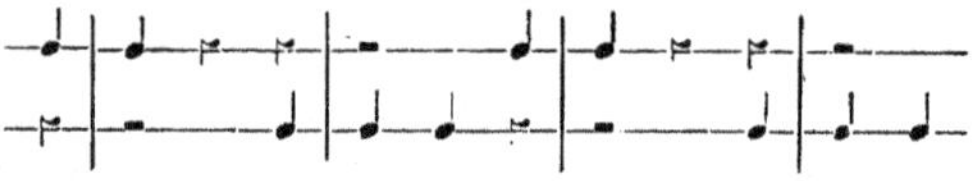

5. Left arm
Right arm

etc., etc.

In 5 the left arm after the 3rd bar should be slightly raised again beat 1.

Note.—If the rest-value leaves sufficient time for the exercise to be do only, new lines of movement are formed, *e.g.* :

The arm should connect the position of beat 1 with the position of beat 3, line forming a quadrant of a circle:—

PHRASING WITH THE FEET.

6.

7.

8.

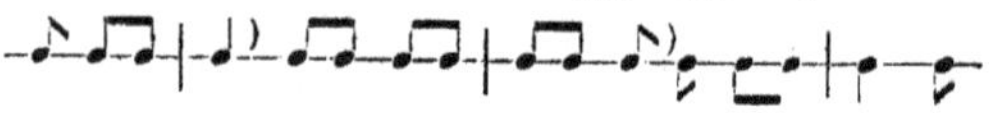

More difficult exercises.—Repeat the above exercises, adding various ways of phrasing with the arms.

PERIODS FORMED BY PHRASES PUNCTUATED BY RESTS OR BY CONTRASTING THEMES.

9. The cæsura can be made: (*a*) by rests; (*b*) by longer notes; (*c*) by shorter notes, forming a contrast:—

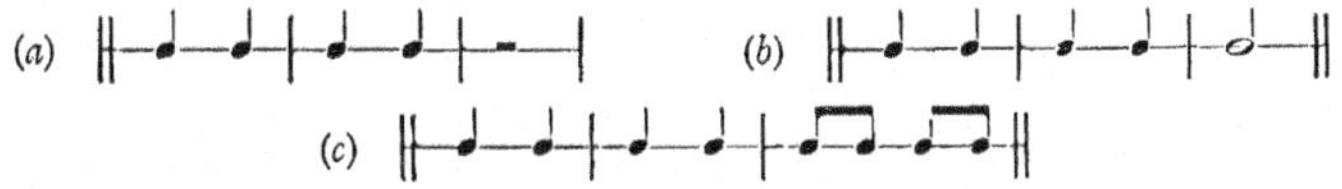

10. The pupil should note whether there is a dotted-minim rest or a dotted minim (𝅗𝅥.):—

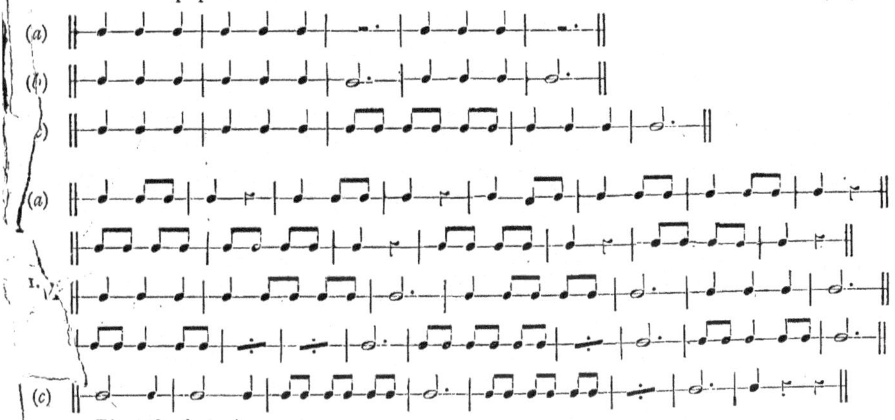

Fine (final stop).

ANALYSIS OF NOTE-VALUES.

TRIPLE AND ONE-THIRD VALUES.

DOTTED MINIM 𝅗𝅥.

Execution: Beat 1, the step; Beat 2, cross the free leg over the supporting leg; Beat 3, resume position 1. The free leg makes the fresh step.

The arms beat 3. On beat 2 the head is inclined in the opposite direction from that of the crossed leg.

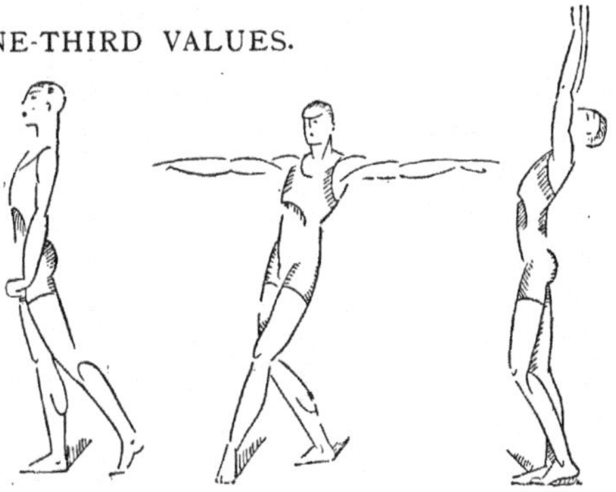

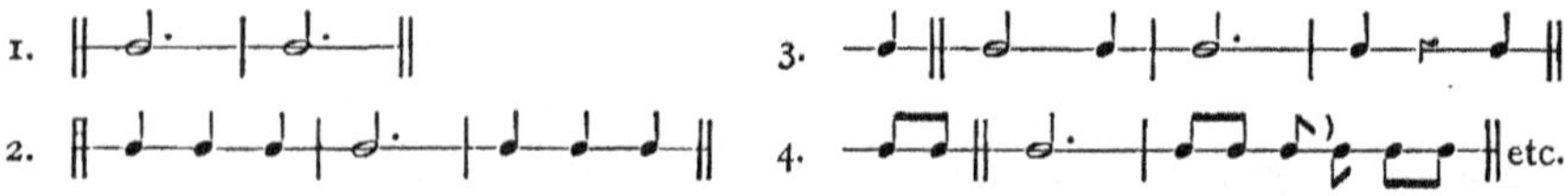

DOTTED CROTCHET ♩.   THREE QUAVERS ♪♪♪

If the feet walk three steps ♪♪♪ while the arm beats one crotchet, a dot must be placed after this crotchet. The time-signature for a bar of compound duple time is $\frac{6}{8}$; for compound triple, $\frac{9}{8}$:—

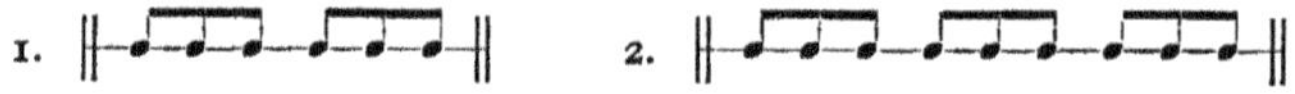

ANACRUSIC FORMS.

Combinations of ♪♪♪ *and of* ♩.

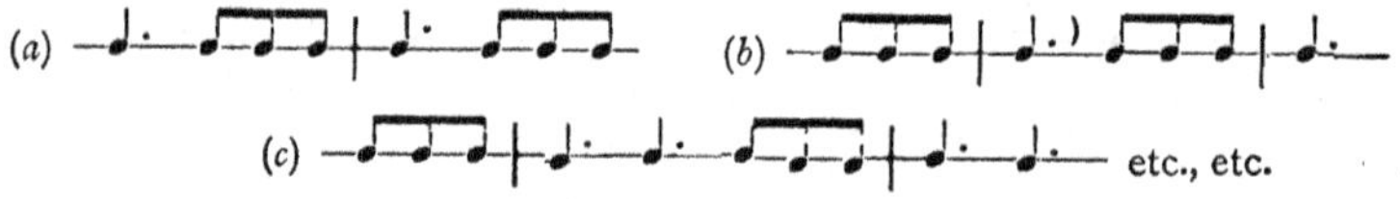

♩. + ♩. = 𝅗𝅥.   ♩ + ♩ + ♩ = 𝅗𝅥.

Twice the length of ♩. is 𝅗𝅥.

The 𝅗𝅥. can therefore be expressed by three movements ♩ ♩ ♩ = 𝅗𝅥. or with two movements ♩. ♩. = 𝅗𝅥.

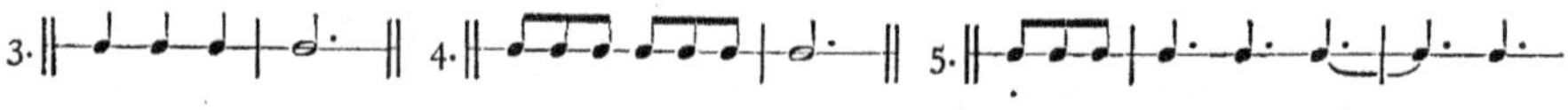

𝅝⁝

The note 𝅝⁝ formed by ♩. ⁀ ♩. ⁀ ♩. is expressed by the same three movements as 𝅗𝅥. in $\frac{3}{4}$:—

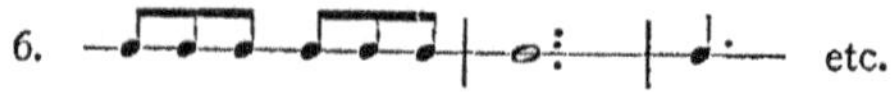

TRIPLET ♪♪♪ (3)

Neither the 𝅗𝅥 nor the ♩ should be dotted unless these periods are regularly and continuously divided into three. When this division is exceptional, no dot is put. If in $\frac{2}{4}$ or $\frac{3}{4}$ a beat is divided as an exception into ♪♪♪ the figure 3 is placed over or under this *triplet*. If in $\frac{6}{8}$ or $\frac{9}{8}$ time a beat is divided as an exception into two quavers ♫, a 2 is placed over or under this *duplet*:—

Difficult exercises.—Three ♪'s which follow one another without a break form a little bar of $\frac{3}{8}$ time. From this new forms of syncopation arise ♪|♩ and ♩|♪

SYNCOPATION ♪|♩ ♩|♪

The arm-beat coincides with the knee-bend:—

Combinations, with different phrasings:—

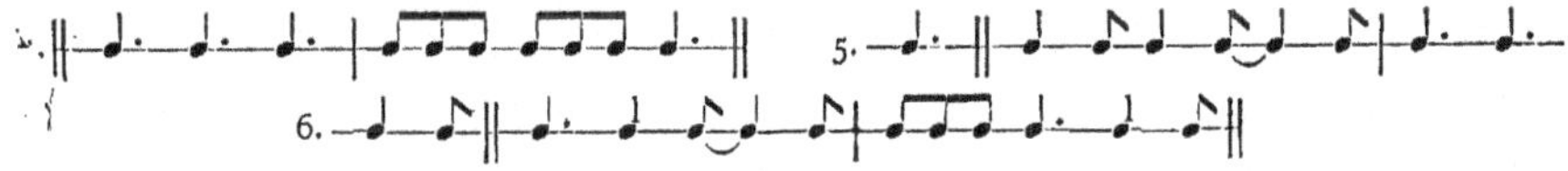

SIX WAYS OF SKIPPING.—(*See* diagrams, p. 36.)

1. Free leg:—Raise the thigh horizontally.
2. „ Stretch out the leg in front.
3. „ Cross the leg in front.
4. „ Bend the knee backward.
5. „ Stretch the leg behind.
6. „ Cross the leg behind.

The supporting leg makes two consecutive springs.

Whenever a rhythm composed of a long note followed by a short one is expressed several times in succession in quick time |♩ ♪♩ ♪♩ ♪| *or* |♩ ♪♩ ♪| it is well to use the skipping step, that is to say, to interpret it by two springs on the same foot.

Simple groups of two equal notes of which the first is very much accentuated can also be interpreted by the skipping step. *Example:*— 

TO BE INTERPRETED WITH THE SIX WAYS OF SKIPPING.

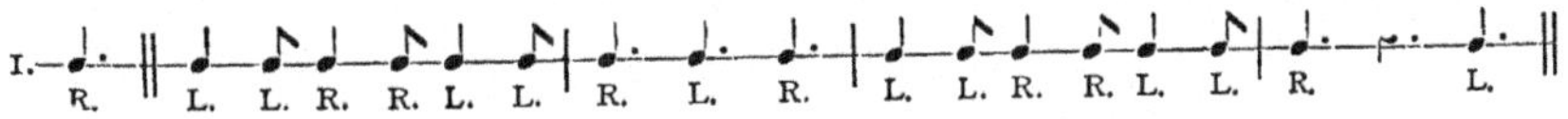

2. 3.

Accentuation mark: Λ

4. 5.

etc.

1st way.

2nd way.

3rd way.

4th way.

5th way.

6th way.

THREE TIMES AS FAST AND THREE TIMES AS SLOW.

$\frac{3}{8}$, $\frac{9}{8}$, $\frac{27}{8}$.

(a) If we take a bar of $\frac{9}{8}$  three times as slow we get a bar of $\frac{27}{8}$ 

(b) If we take a bar of $\frac{27}{8}$ three times as fast we get a bar of $\frac{9}{8}$, and by taking this three times as fast we get a bar of $\frac{3}{8}$ 

The pupil will interpret these three time-values by steps and gestures of varying length and amplitude :—

1*a*. Three bars  then three bars 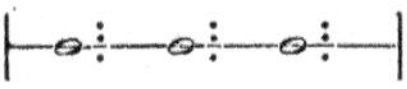

2*a*. Three bars  then three bars 

1*b*. and 2*b*. Repeat the exercises 1*a* and 2*a*, making 3 steps for each beat:—

3. Three bars ; then three ; then three ; then three ; then three 

See page 12: *The five lengths of step,* and pages 8 and 10, the vertical and horizontal ...es of movement.

4. *More difficult exercise.*—Syncopation. The arms beat 3:—

UNEQUAL BARS.

Changes of time may also be made by arranging the bars in a manner similar to the given examples:—

♩=♩ $\frac{2}{4}$ and $\frac{3}{4}$ ♩.=♩. $\frac{6}{8}$ and $\frac{9}{8}$

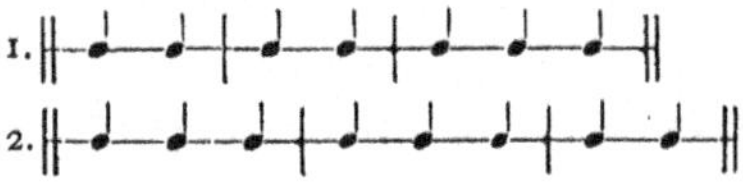

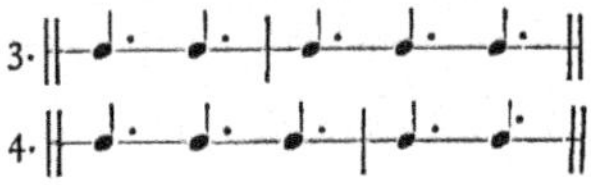

♪=♪ $\frac{3}{4}$ and $\frac{6}{8}$

5. *(a)*  *(b)* 

as well as all the combinations with ♩ ♪ *or* ♪ ♩ *or* 𝅗𝅥 etc.

In Example 5 note that for the first time we find beats of *varying lengths* (unequal beats).

Rhythms with unequal bars and unequal beats:—

6.  7. 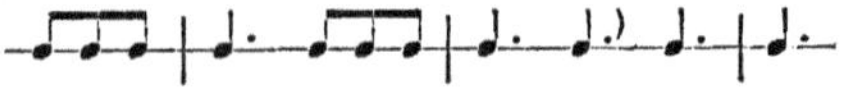

8. 

BREATHING.

Use only those rhythms which can be conveniently interpreted by breathing, *e.g.* :—

1. 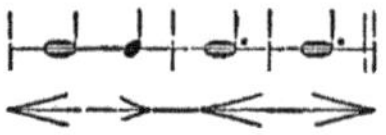 2. 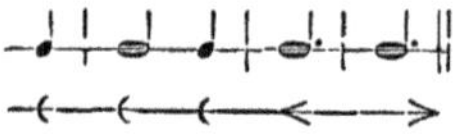 etc.

See Chapter 2, page 27.

INFLUENCE OF BREATHING ON MOVEMENTS.

(*a*) Take a deep breath, at the same time raising the arms in such a way as to suggest that they have been forced upward.

(*b*) Ditto, but the breathing now coincides with the raising of the thigh (or the head).

(*c*) Ditto, with trunk bending forward, backward, or sideways.

(*d*) Ditto, with kneeling or rising.

(*e*) Ditto, with a step forward, backward, or sideways, etc.

(*f*) Combine gestures and movements evoked by the act of breathing with gestures and movements of other parts of the body, *e.g.*, shoulders, arms, trunk, legs, head, hips, hands, etc.

(*g*) Make any gesture (*see* Vol. II., page 59. *The 20 Gestures*); then take a deep breath, thereby increasing its range.

(*h*) Take a deep breath, make any gesture or movement, then breathe out so as to produce a *descrescendo* of muscular action.

These exercises should be continued in each of the lessons of the succeeding chapters.

In a general way it may be said that in every realisation the phrase begins with breathing-in and ends with breathing-out.

EXERCISES FOR INDEPENDENCE OF MOVEMENT.

1. Same direction: The two limbs 

2. Contrasting force: One limb *forte*
The other *piano* 

3. Movements varying in extent :—

The two limbs 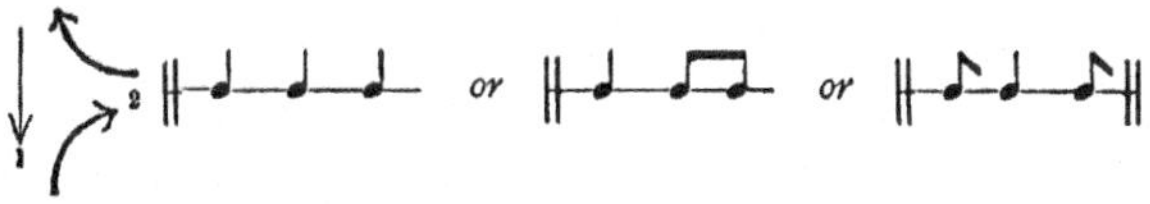

(One gesture larger than the other.)

4. *Movements varying in length of time.*—Repeat Exercises 1, 2, and 3: one limb two or three times as fast as the other (one limb completing the gesture in three beats, the other in one beat).

The figures 1, 2, and 3 shown on the lines of No. 3 apply to the notes, not to the beats.

Contrary Movements :—

5. One limb  the other  and vice-versa.

6. One limb 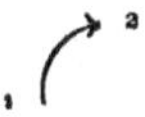 the other 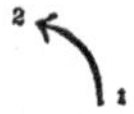 and vice-versa.

7. One limb  the other 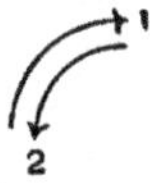 and vice-versa.

8. One limb 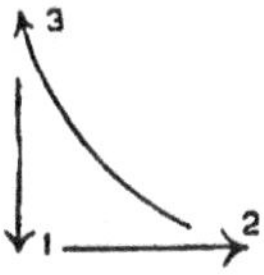 the other 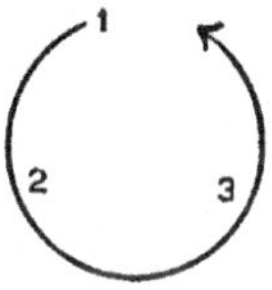 *or* 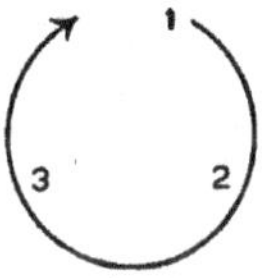 etc., and vice-versa.

EXERCISES FOR CONTROL AND INHIBITION.

1. The pupils walk  At the command *hopp*, given by one of them, they walk twice as fast or twice as slow.

2. The pupils walk  The same as No. 1, but three times as fast or as slow.

Repeat with combinations of different notes, such as 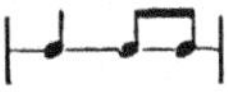 *or*  *or*  *or*  etc., etc.

3. The pupils walk  and at the *hopp* they add an unaccented step (weak beat) to these two crotchets, indicating this last beat by a turn of the wrist.

(*a*) They then return to $\frac{2}{4}$

(*b*). They continue in $\frac{3}{4}$  and at the next *hopp* omit the gesture and the step of the third beat and begin walking in $\frac{2}{4}$ again.

Example:

4. The pupils walk  At *hopp* they beat  and walk  etc.

5. The pupils make the following movements with both arms:—

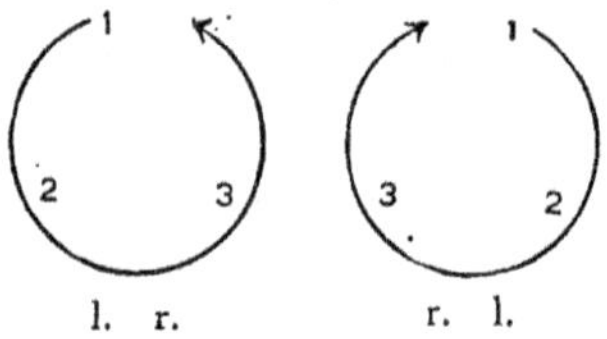

and at *hopp*

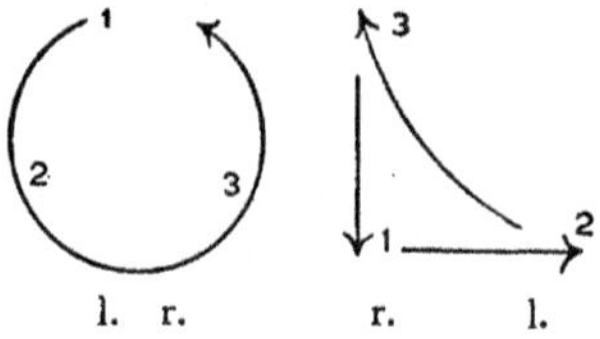

Exercises in Hearing.—1. The teacher plays a theme three times. At the fourth repetition the pupils realise it, *either by clapping or by stepping:*—

Example:

2. The teacher writes a theme on the board, *e.g.*  and plays it three times with certain nuances, *e.g.*:—

First time *f* | ——— | *f* ———

Second „ *pp* | ——— | *p* ——— etc., etc.

or with accents on certain notes, *e.g.*,  At the fourth repetition the pupils realise the theme, showing the nuances.

3. The teacher plays in ♪'s. The pupils reply in ♩'s or in ♩.'s.

Example: Teacher

Pupils

etc.

4. The teacher plays 4 bars of 𝅗𝅥's. The pupils interpret the third and fourth bars, the *tempo* being first time *Moderato*, the second time *Allegro*, the third time *Lento*, etc., *ad libitum*.

Example: Teacher

Pupils

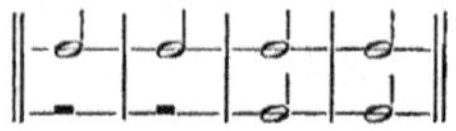

Then the pupils divide the third and fourth bar into 

Example : 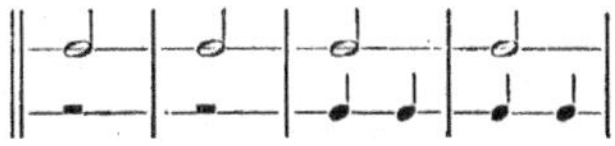

When the teacher plays *Allegro* or *Presto* the pupil must at once bring the weight of the body forward, and when the teacher plays *Lento* the pupils must transfer the weight of the body backward.

5. The same exercise with 𝅗𝅥.'s:—

Teacher
Pupils

6. The teacher plays four ♪'s in varying *tempi*. The pupils at once realise them:—

Teacher
Pupils

etc., etc.

The pupils write on the blackboard or in their note-books the rhythms studied during the lesson.

FREE EXERCISES.

Syncopation in 3 time:—

X
Y
Z

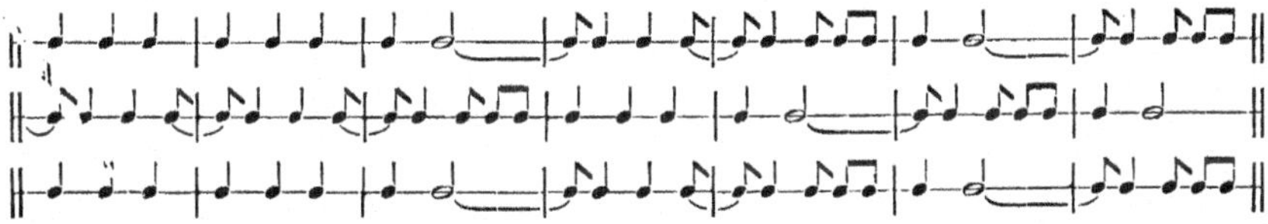

The pupils form three parallel lines:—

and realise in this position bars 1, 3, and 6, whilst for bars 4, 5, and 7 they are grouped as follows:—

X, Y, and *Z* take hands, and the syncopations must be stepped so as to make it appear that the pupil in the rear is drawn forward by the other two (or that the two pupils in the rear are drawn forward by the pupil in the middle).

Thus the pupil in the rear make syncopation by retardation (weight of the body thrown backward), the pupils walking in front make syncopation by anticipation (weight of body forward).

IMPROVISATION.

The teacher asks a pupil to improvise:—

1. Two bars of $\frac{2}{4}$ introducing a syncopated note.
2. Three bars of [illegible] n a bar of $\frac{6}{8}$
3. Four bars [illegible] n two cæsuras.
4. Two bars to be repeated immediately, twice as fast or twice as slow.

EXERCISES IN CONDUCTING.

1. A pupil beats time, introducing unequal bars.
2. A pupil beats time, introducing rests.
3. A pupil beats bars, sometimes *forte* sometimes *piano*, and the other pupils follow the beating.

See: 1st *Marches Rythmiques* Nos. 3—7, Edition Jobin & Co., No. 780.
2nd *Esquisses Rythmiques pour piano*, Edition Jobin & Co., No. 1528.

CHAPTER III.

QUADRUPLE TIME.

EXERCISES IN WALKING WITHOUT BEATING TIME.

The four beats

Anacrusic forms :—

EXERCISES IN WALKING WHILE BEATING TIME.

PREPARATORY EXERCISE.

From 1 to 2. The arms are crossed lightly over the chest.

„ 2 to 3. The arms are extended sideways in a horizontal direction.

„ 3 to 4. The arms are lightly raised.

„ 4 to 1. The arms are lowered strongly with accentuation at the point 1.

See page 7. *Lines of Movement.*

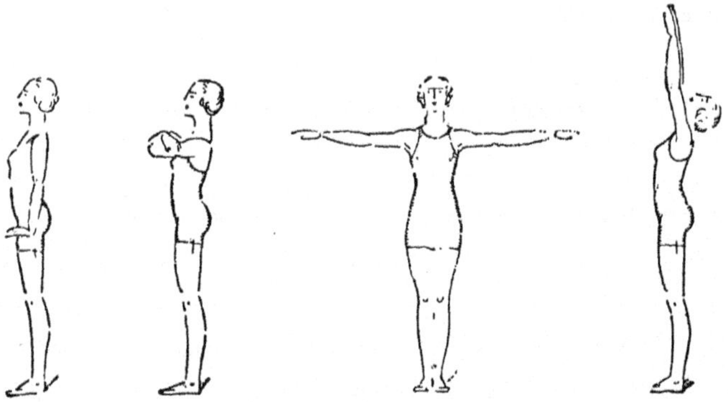

Beat 1. Beat 2. Beat 3. Beat 4.

the crusic and anacrusic bars written above, *beating time.*

PHRASES AND RESTS.

PHRASING WITH THE ARMS.

1. Right arm
   Left arm

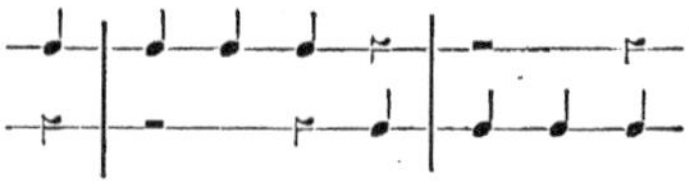

2. Right arm
   Left arm

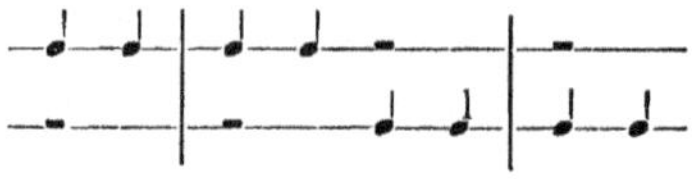

The Rest ▬

3.

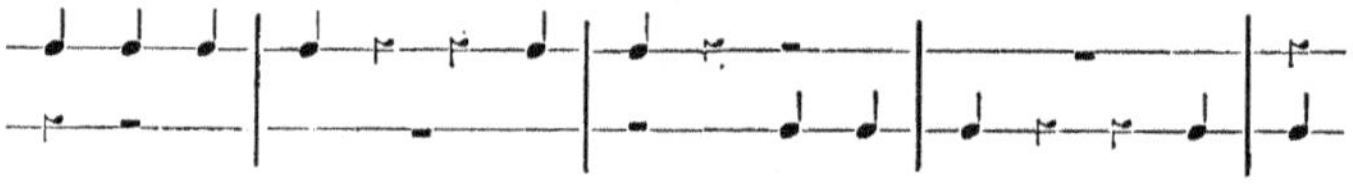

Realisation of Rests.—The arms retain the position they were in during the realisation of the last note before the rest, then after the rest they take up the preparatory position for the note which follows.

PHRASING WITH THE FEET.

4.

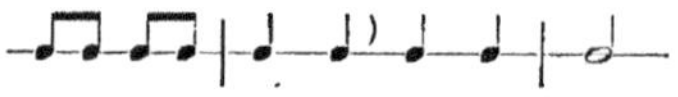

5.

6.

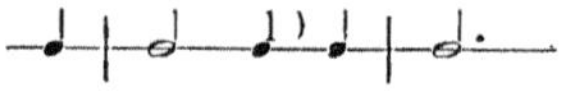

(Eventually the arms can phrase alternately with the feet.)

7. The *cæsura*, or rather the period of rest which separates two phrases or one phrase and its repetition, can be made in various ways :—

(*a*) By a rest.
(*b*) By a change of time.
(*c*) By a new rhythm.
(*d*) By doubling or halving the speed.

Thus the period of rest may consist simply in a contrast with the time of activity.

3 + 1 = 4 *bars.*

(*a*)

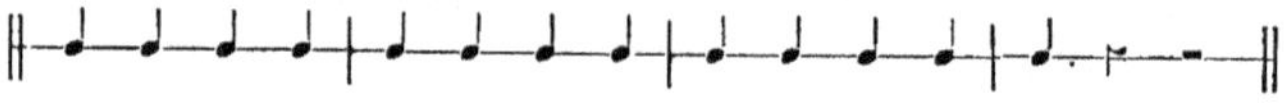

(*b*)

(*c*)

(*d*)

ANALYSIS OF NOTE VALUES.

The Semibreve. 𝅝

Realisation: From 4 to 1. The step.
„ 1 to 2. The free leg is lightly crossed over the supporting leg.
„ 2 to 3. The free leg is stretched out sideways.
„ 3 to 4. The free leg rejoins the supporting leg.

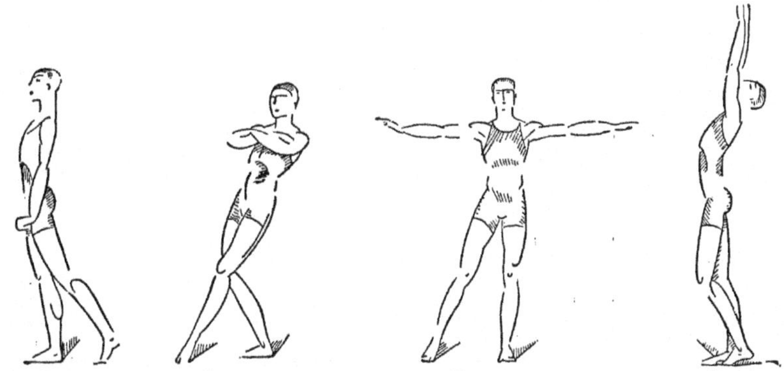

Beat 1. Beat 2. Beat 3. Beat 4.

The quaver rest

DIVISION OF THE SEMIBREVE INTO FOUR OR THREE NOTES OF EQUAL LENGTH.

Semiquaver rest

See page 17: *Grouping of notes.*

When each beat of the bar in 4 time is divided into three (in this case each crotchet is dotted) we get one crusic form and two anacrusic forms:—

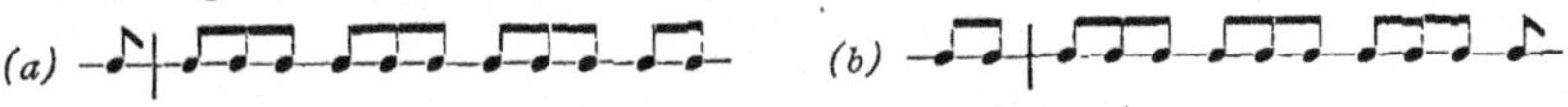

1. 2. 3.

4. ♩. = 𝅝. Realisation as 𝅝 in $\frac{4}{4}$.

The dotted Semibreve 𝅝.

See Vol. II., page 1. Sextuple time.

$\frac{4}{4}$ taken twice as slow $=\frac{4}{2}$ | $\frac{4}{2}$ taken twice as slow $=\frac{4}{1}$

$\frac{4}{4}$ taken twice as fast $=\frac{4}{8}$ | $\frac{4}{8}$ taken twice as fast $=\frac{4}{16}$ 

1. Two bars  then two 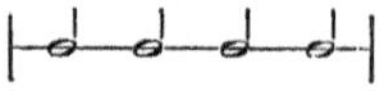
then two 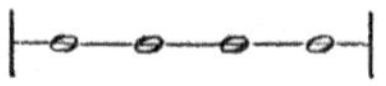

2. Four bars  then four  then four 

3. One bar  then one  etc.

More difficult exercises.—One arm beats 4. The other arm beats 2 in the same lengt of time, *i.e.*, one arm 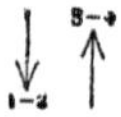 the other arm 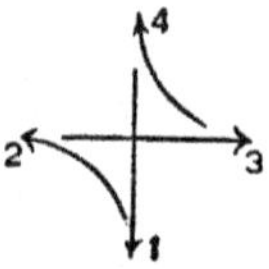

The same exercise, with *syncopation.*

UNEQUAL BARS.

♩ = ♩ $\frac{2}{4}$, $\frac{3}{4}$, and $\frac{4}{4}$

NEW POSSIBILITIES.

1.  2. 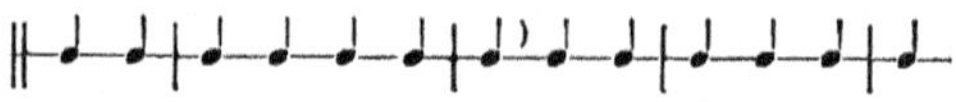

3. 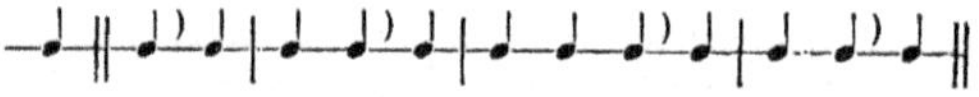

♩. = ♩. $\frac{6}{8}$, $\frac{9}{8}$, and $\frac{12}{8}$

4. 

5. 

𝅘𝅥𝅯 = 𝅘𝅥𝅯 $\frac{3}{4}$ and $\frac{12}{6}$

In $\frac{2}{4}$, $\frac{3}{4}$, $\frac{4}{4}$, each beat consists of four semiquavers. In $\frac{12}{16}$ on the contrary it consists of three () only (see $\frac{12}{8}$).

In $\frac{3}{4}$: 3×4=12 ♬ In $\frac{12}{16}$: 4×3=12 ♬

Notation: 6. (*a*) 

to be realised alternately.

♪=♪ $\frac{3}{2}$ and $\frac{12}{8}$

The same exercise in $\frac{3}{2}$ and $\frac{12}{8}$:—

6. (*b*) 

[A]LTERNATING BARS OF THE SAME LENGTH BUT UNEQUALLY DIVIDED.

7.  8. 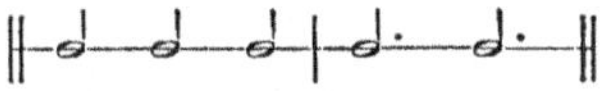

Repeat Exercises 7 and 8, stepping the 𝅗𝅥 without bending.

9.  10. 

11. Step syncopated quavers, beating first in 3, then in 4.

(*a*)  (*b*) 

SKIPPING WITH DIVISION OF THE ♩ INTO FOUR ♬

1. 

See page 35: *Skipping.*

♫ Compared with ♩ ♪

2. 

The rhythm  can also be realised with the skipping step.

SKIPPING WITH ALTERNATE DIVISION OF THE ♩ INTO 3 AND 4.

3. 

× The dot on or under the note ♪ means *staccato*.

4. 

See page 17: *Groupings of notes.*

THE SPRING, STACCATO.

The sign of staccato (a dot above or a dot below the note) means *spring*.

EXERCISES WITH SPRINGING.

1. 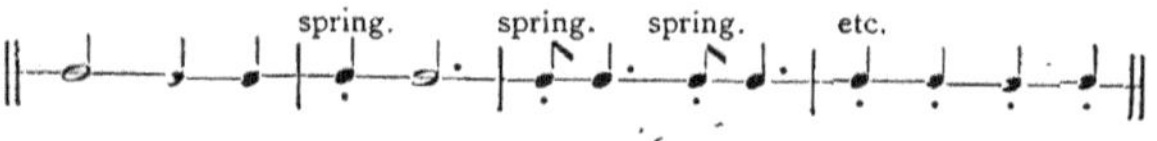

2. 

3. 

etc.

These springs can be made straight up, forward, backward, or to one side, with or without movement of the arms.

In each of the following lessons the teacher should vary some of the exercises, so as to introduce springing.

DIFFERENT WAYS OF GROUPING 8 QUAVERS IN A BAR OF $\frac{3}{4}$.

Unequal beats 3+3+2=8 ♪

1. (*a*)

(*b*)

The third beat of each bar is shorter than the first or second.

3+2+3=8 ♪

2.

𝅗𝅥: ♩. ♩ with a bend on the second beat, 𝅝 is divided into three.

2+3+3=8 ♪

3.

etc.

BREATHING.

Of the rhythms given in this chapter, use only those which are easily adapted to breathing:—

Example: 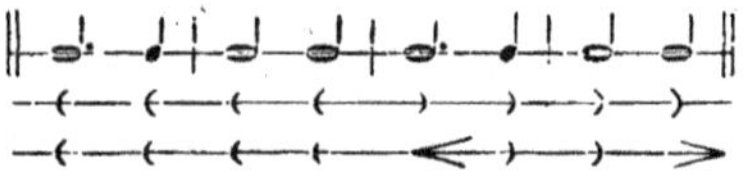

INDEPENDENCE OF MOVEMENT.

1. One arm beats 6/8, the other 3/4 in the same length of time:—

Right arm
Left arm

two against three.

The teacher can play quavers.

MORE DIFFICULT EXERCISES.

2. 3/4 and 12/8 in the same length of time:—

Right arm
Left arm

three against four.

3. Three bars 2/4, two bars 3/4 in the same length of time:—

Right arm
Left arm

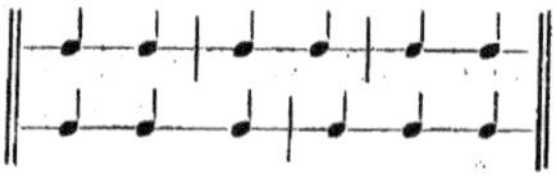

4. Four bars of 9/8, three bars of 12/8 in the same length of time:—

Right arm
Left arm

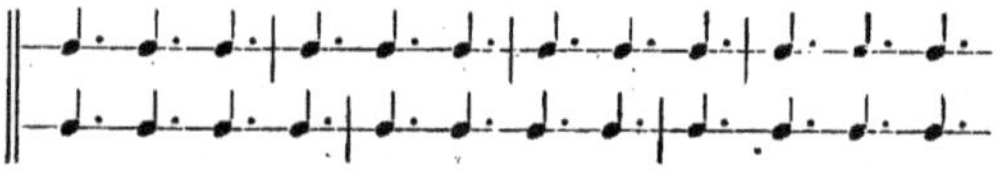

CONTROL AND INHIBITION.

1. Changes of bar by prolonging the length of the anacrusis:—

2. By shortening the anacrusis:— 

etc.

3. By taking twice or three times as fast or slow :—

(a) 

(b) 

4. By omission of a beat :—

5. The pupil walks |♩ ♩ ♩ ♩|. At *hopp*, he kneels and counts (*i.e.*, realises in thought) two or four bars, then gets up and continues walking.

N.B.—If the *hopp* is given on the third beat, the bars will be counted ♩|♩ ♩ ♩

If the *hopp* is given on the second beat, the bars will be counted ♩ ♩|♩ ♩

If the *hopp* is given on the first beat, the bars will be counted ♩ ♩ ♩|♩

Example: 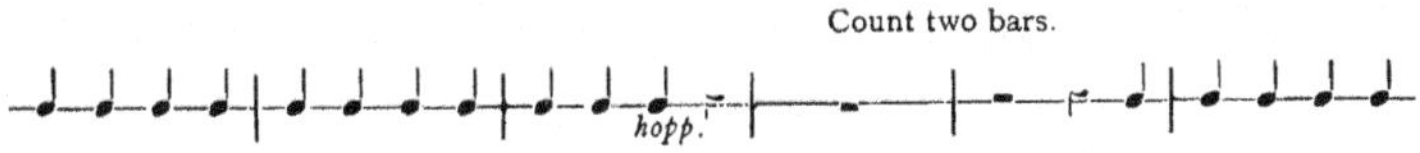

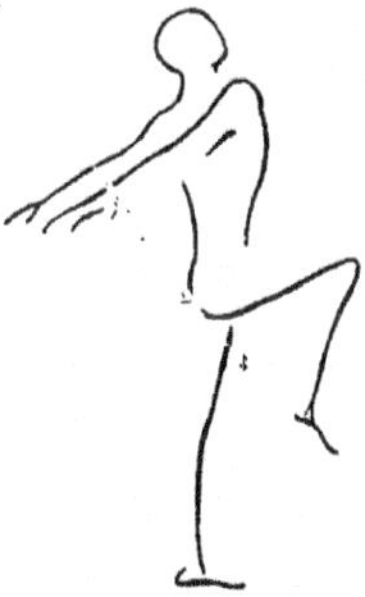

6. The pupil walks |♫ ♫ ♫ ♫|. At *hopp* he stands still, raises himself on the toes of one foot, lifts the knee of the other leg, and twists the trunk in the direction opposite to that of the supporting leg. The leg and arms follow the movement of the trunk. He remains two bars in this position.

The pupil walks |♩ ♩ ♩ ♩|. At *hopp*, a spring forward, backward or sideways.

EXERCISES IN HEARING.

1. The teacher plays one bar which the pupils immediately realise. While they realise it, the teacher plays another bar, etc.; this makes a two-part canon between pianoforte and pupil.

First voice = the teacher. Second voice = the pupil.

2. The pupil walks When the teacher plays on one of the beats, the pupil steps on the next beat. The same with etc.

N.B.—The pupils write down the rhythms studied during the lesson.

ANALYSIS OF NOTE VALUES.

The teacher plays four 's. When he reaches the third the pupils realise it with him, also the fourth; or in the same way they step two bars 's, 's or any rhythm given beforehand.

1. Teacher / Pupils
2. Teacher / Pupils
3. Teacher / Pupils
4. Teacher / Pupils
5. Teacher / Pupils
6. Teacher / Pupils

IMPROVISATION.

Several pupils are chosen to improvise one bar each in immediate succession. The class then realises the whole phrase.

The teacher asks, for example, for:—

1. Three bars of $\frac{4}{4}$ without an anacrusis.
2. Four bars of $\frac{12}{8}$ beginning with an anacrusis on 4.
3. A thetic bar of

The same, twice as slow

„ in the original *tempo*

„ twice as fast

4. A thetic bar of 9/8

The same, three times as fast = 3/8

„ in the original *tempo* = 9/8

„ three times as slow = 27/8

EXERCISES IN CONDUCTING PHRASES.

A pupil stands facing the class. While conducting he signs first to one pupil then to another to come out of line and walk round the hall:—

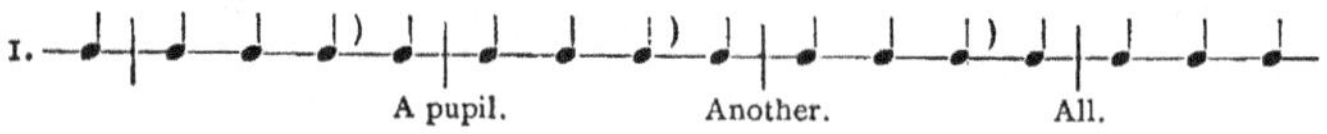

2. With  as anacrusis:—

FREE EXERCISES.

TABLE OF THE VARIOUS TIME-VALUES.

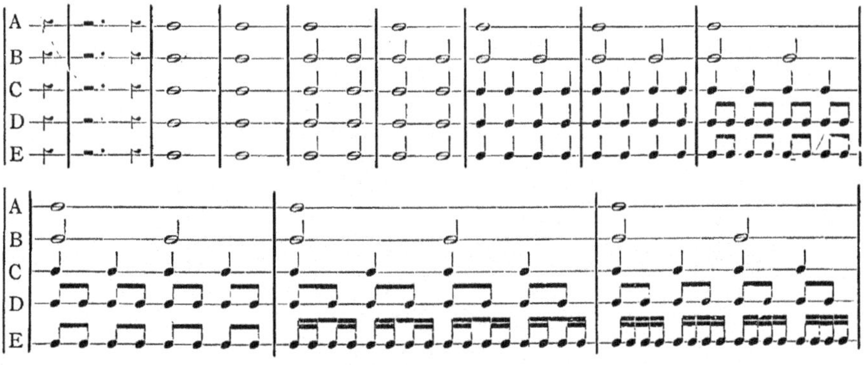

The pupils form five concentric circles, A, B, C, D, E, each facing in an opposite direction. They all kneel on one knee with bowed heads. They begin beating time on the fourth beat, , and rise on the fourth beat of the following bar. At the end  they kneel on the first beat, then on the first beat of the next bar they stop beating time and bow their heads.

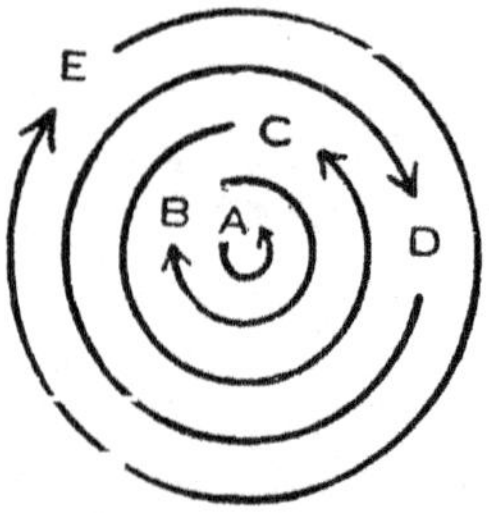

See : 1. *Marches rythmiques*, Nos. 8 to 16 (Edition : Jobin & Cie., No. 780).
2. *Esquisses rythmiques* (Edition : Jobin & Cie., No. 1528).

CHAPTER IV.

QUINTUPLE TIME.

EXERCISES IN MARCHING WHILE BEATING TIME.

Preparatory Exercise.

From 1 to 2. Cross the arms over the chest.
,, 2 to 3. Stretch them out horizontally in front.
,, 3 to 4. Stretch them sideways.
,, 4 to 5. Raise them vertically.
,, 5 to 1. Lower them energetically with accentuation on the beat 1.

Beat 1.

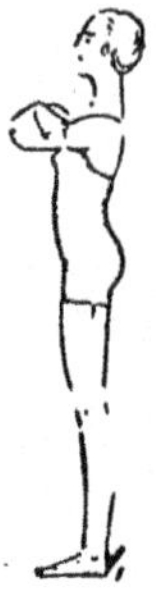

Beat 2.

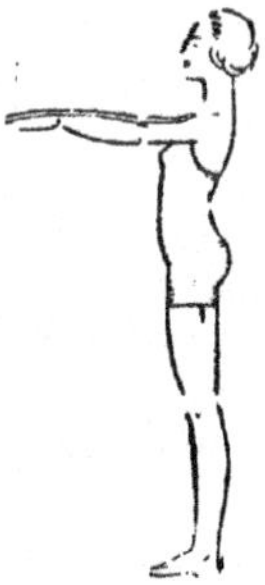

Beat 3.

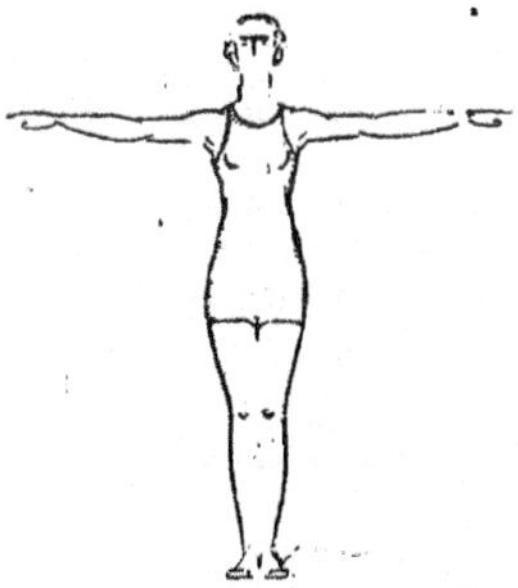

Beat 4.

Beat 5.

$\frac{15}{8}$

4.  and fourteen anacrusic forms,

 etc.

PHRASES AND RESTS.

PHRASING WITH THE ARMS.

1. Left / Right 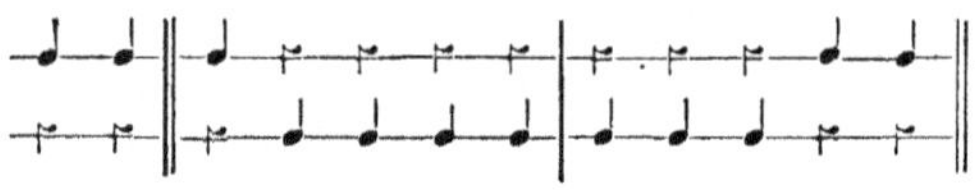 etc.

PHRASING WITH THE FEET.

2. 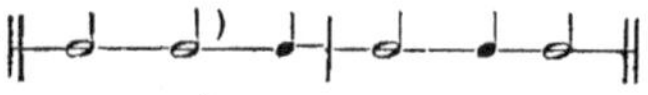

3. 

See page 16: *Ways of Phrasing.*

MORE DIFFICULT FORM.

4. Secondary accentuation of the ♩ in $\frac{5}{4}$. One arm beats two unequal beats, the other beats five equal beats in the same length of time.

(*a*) One Arm / The other  (*b*) One Arm / The other 

The feet step the given rhythm.

5. Periods of two themes, A and B, freely interchanging and finishing with a rest, or with some bar forming a contrast and so giving an impression of a rest (*see* page 44), *e.g.* :—

Theme A  Theme B 

Final bar of rest 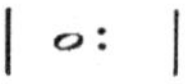

Four bars 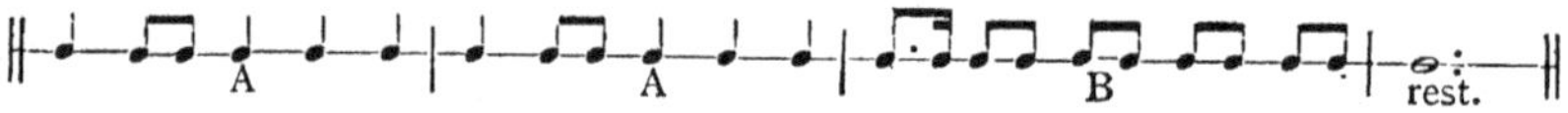

Other examples :—

(*a*)	A	B	B	rest.
(*b*)	A	B	A	"

Five bars (*a*)	A	A	A	B	rest
(*b*)	A	A	B	B	,,
(*c*)	A	B	A	B	,,
(*d*)	A	B	B	B	,,
(*e*)	A	B	B	A	,,
(*f*)	A	A	B	A	,,
(*g*)	A	B	A	A	,,

In realising these periods the pupils may change their direction after the bar of rest.

Other rhythms:—

ANALYSIS OF NOTE VALUES.

Five times and one-fifth values.

$\frac{5}{4}$ o : The note of 5 beats :—

Realisation.—5 to 1. The step.

1 to 2. Cross the free leg over the supporting leg.

2 to 3. Stretch the free leg out in front bending the supporting leg.

3 to 4. Extend the free leg to one side.

4 to 5. Bring the free leg back to supporting leg.

Beat 1. Beat 2. Beat 3. Beat 4. Beat 5.

$\frac{15}{8}$ = 𝅝 · · ·

Same realisation as 𝅝 :

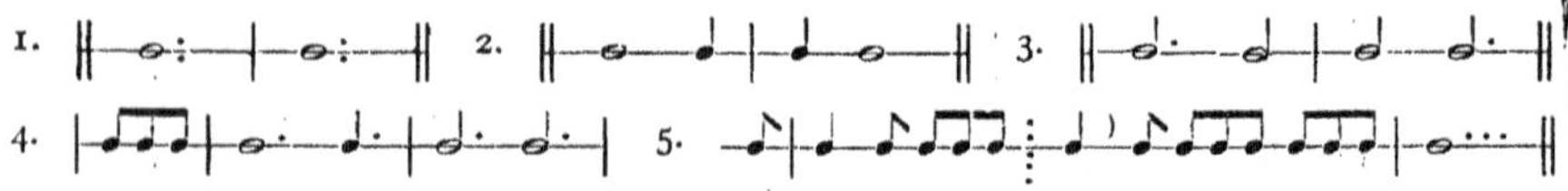

DIVISION OF BARS IN 2 AND 4 TIME INTO UNEQUAL GROUPS OF QUAVERS.

The total number of quavers is nine = $\frac{9}{8}$

5+4=9 ♪

4+5=9 ♪

2+2+2+3 =9 ♪

other

(a) One Arm ... OF THE BAR IN 2 TIME.

The oth...

NEW FORM ... forms

$\frac{10}{8}$

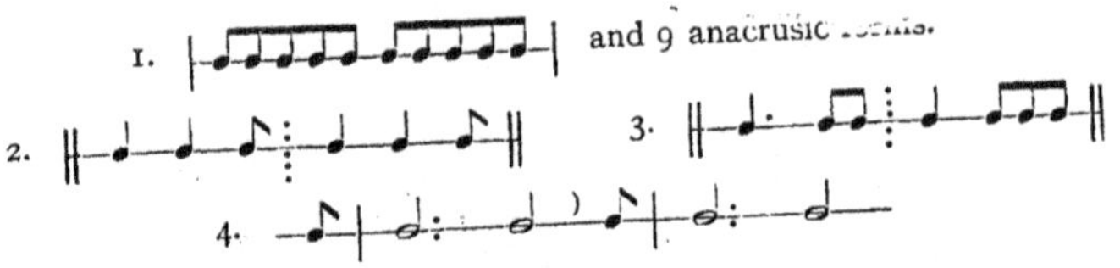

𝅗𝅥 : =5 ♪

The 𝅗𝅥 : and 𝅗𝅥 are not to be subdivided.

GROUPINGS OF TEN QUAVERS IN BARS OF 3 AND 4 TIME.

Groups of quavers forming unequal beats:—

2+2+3+3=10 ♪

+ 3 + 2 = 10

NEW FORM OF THE BAR IN 3 TIME.

15/8 making 3 time.

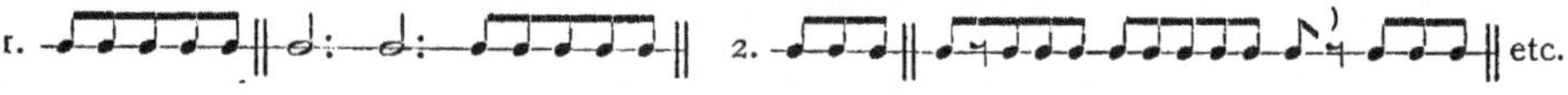

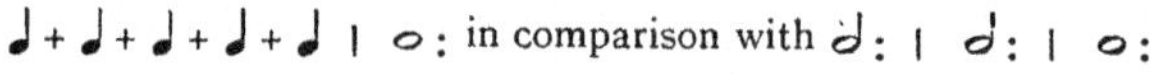

The  can be beaten in 2 time 

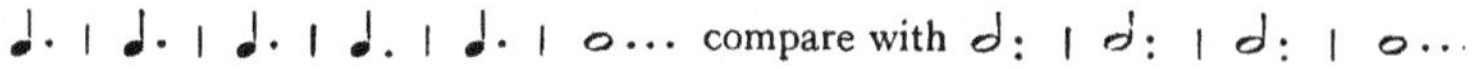

The can be beaten in 3 time 

These two last forms will be used by the teacher in writing down new rhythms for the pupils to interpret :—

DIVISION OF EQUAL NOTES INTO 2, 3, 4, 5, SHORTER NOTES OF EQUAL VALUE.

 is longer than 

SYNCOPATIONS.

Rapid syncopations can be interpreted by springing.

UNEQUAL BARS.

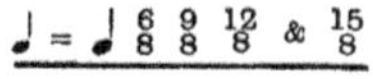

3. Repeat each bar twice.

The same in the reverse order.

RHYTHMS COMPOSED OF UNEQUAL BARS.

PLASTIC COUNTERPOINT.

The teacher plays a rhythm containing 𝅗𝅥, 𝅗𝅥., 𝅝, 𝅝:, 𝅗𝅥: and ♩

The pupils step only the beats which are not played, *i.e.*:—

The second beat of the 𝅗𝅥.

The second and third beats of the 𝅗𝅥.

The second, third and fourth beats of the 𝅝 etc.

e.g.:

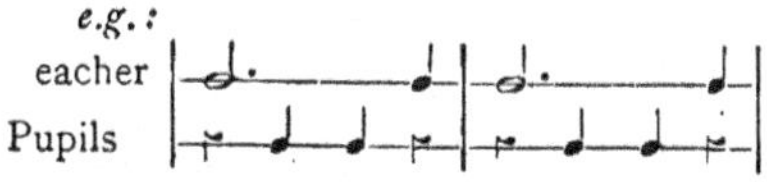

2. 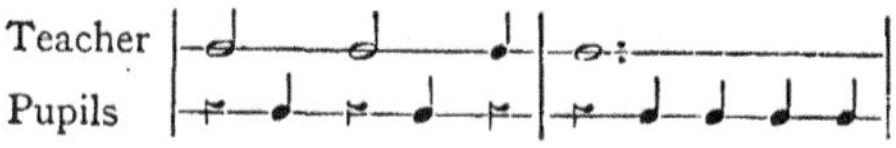

etc., etc.

This is called *counterpoint in crotchets.*

The following is *counterpoint in quavers:*

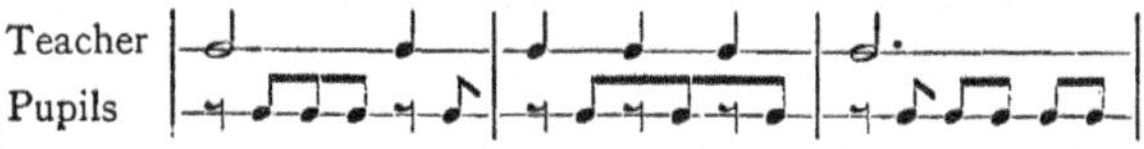

Counterpoint in semiquavers:

Instead of stepping the notes of the counterpoint, the pupil may realise them by gestures of the arm or hand, or, in slow music, by movements of the head or by *breathing*.

BREATHING.

Use only those rhythms which are suitable for breathing.

Example:— 

INDEPENDENCE OF THE LIMBS.

1. $\frac{3}{4}$ beaten in canon.

(*a*) Right arm / Left arm 

(*b*) Left arm / Right arm 

2. $\frac{4}{4}$ in canon.

3. $\frac{5}{4}$ in canon.

MORE DIFFICULT EXERCISES.

4. $\frac{10}{8}$ Right arm / Left arm 

2 against 5.

5. $\frac{15}{8}$ Left arm / Right arm 

3 against 5.

Repeat the same exercises with arms and feet.

CONTROL.

1. From $\frac{2}{4}$ to $\frac{5}{4}$ and back to $\frac{2}{4}$ at *hopp*.

2. Walk at $\frac{5}{4}$. At *hopp* walk in syncopation and *vice-versâ*.

3. $\frac{15}{8}$; at *hopp* walk in syncopation and *vice-versâ*.

4.  at *hopp* stand still, but continue the movement in thought—at *hopp*, walk again.

5. The same exercise, but the teacher plays o:, and the pupils divide this o: in thought into fifteen quavers. At *hopp* they finish the bar, stepping the necessary number of quavers, *e.g.*, if the teacher says *hopp* on the seventh quaver, the pupils end the bar by stepping eight quavers.

6. The teacher gives a rhythm, *e.g.*,  Then he plays two o:'s, at the third o: the pupils realise the given rhythm in the exact *tempo* in which the teacher played the o: The teacher should vary the *tempo*—*presto, allegro, moderato, andante, adagio, lento.*

7. The pupils walk ♩ in any given time. The teacher calls *two, three, four* or *five,* and the pupils run the required number of steps during the next beat.

The pupils memorize the rhythm thus formed, and eventually realise it without any word of command from the teacher.

EXERCISES IN HEARING.

Realisation: 1.  etc.

2. The teacher plays ♩ The pupils answer by walking in syncopation.

3. The pupils are divided into several groups, each group representing plastically a different note-value.

E.g.: Group 1 represents ♩.; group 2, ♪; group 3, 𝅗𝅥.; group 4, ; group 5,  etc.

The pupils of each group take hands. When the teacher plays quavers on the pianoforte, group 2 starts running, the leader choosing his direction at will. If the teacher plays with the right hand 𝅗𝅥., and with the left hand , groups 3 and 5 begin to move simultaneously.

N.B.—The pupils should write down the rhythms studied in the lesson.

IMPROVISATION.

The teacher asks a pupil to improvise.

1. Three bars of different lengths in duple time, *e.g.:* $\frac{2}{4}$, $\frac{6}{8}$, and $\frac{10}{8}$.
2. Four bars in $\frac{5}{4}$ time with 2 cæsuras (therefore 3 phrases).
3. Six bars with lengthened anacrusis.

EXERCISES IN CONDUCTING.

A pupil conducts the class, introducing one or more of the following:—

1. Rests. 2. Twice as fast and twice as slow. 3. Three times as fast and three times as slow. 4. Walking backward, then forward. 5. Springs. 6. Pathetic accents. 7. Division of the class into small groups:—

e.g.: 

FREE EXERCISES.

Syncopation in couples:—

The pupils (in couples) face one another, all lunging forward with arms raised and hands pressed against their partners'. In the four first bars:—

(*Z*) The pressure of the hands remains steady.
(Y) „ „ „ „ increases so that *Z* of necessity walks back, and Y walks forward. At the fourth bar Y *decrescendo, Z crescendo,* on the spot.

The couples can walk in a straight line:

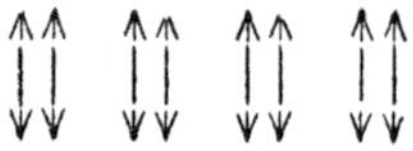

Or one behind the other:

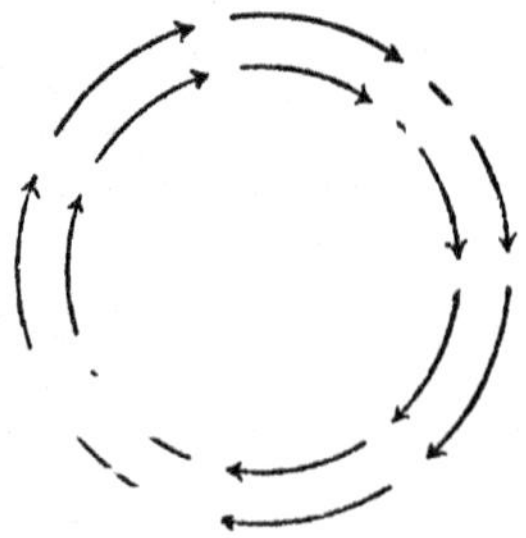

See: (*i.*) *Marche Rythmiques* Nos. 17 to 22 (Jobin's Edition, No. 780).
(*ii*) *Exercices de plastique animée* (Jobin's Edition, No. 1528).

THE PRICES QUOTED IN THIS LIST ARE THE OLD PRICES.

E. JAQUES-DALCROZE.

VOCAL WORKS WITH ENGLISH TEXT

CHILDREN- AND ACTION-SONGS

FOR ONE OR TWO VOICES OR IN UNISON.

The prices here given are subject to an increase of 30 per cent., except in the cases of the Five Publications marked thus * the prices of which already include the increases.

No.		s.	d.
808.	Four Children-Songs and Dances. Op. 34	5	0

Sixteen Part-songs for Medium Voice and Pianoforte, with explanatory text.

1. Diddle, diddle dee.
2. The merry Huntsmen.
3. Sir Cuckoo's marriage.
4. The lake.
5. My Pussy Cat.
6. The bonny Baby.
7. Come, let us dance.
8. Just like this.
9. The bashful boy.
10. The snow-white lambkin.
11. Santa Claus.
12. Johnny's ride.
13. My heart is thine.
14. The naughty little boy.
15. Washing Day.
16. The Willow Tree.

No.		s.	d.
809.	New Children-Songs and Dances. Op. 37	5	0

Fifteen Part-songs for Medium Voice and Pianoforte, with explanatory text.

1. Song of the good little birds.
2. Song of the old grannies.
3. Song of the new skirt.
4. Song of the obliging shopwoman.
5. Song of the Seasons.
6. Song of the little dwarfs.
7. Song of the child who won't eat his food.
8. Song of the bridal pair.
9. Song of the Doctor's visit.
10. Song of the bleating lambkin.
11. Song of the brave little soldiers.
12. Song of the little prisoner.
13. Song of the little doggie.
14. Song of the kind maiden.
15. Song of the good workmen.

No.		s.	d.
810.	Children-songs. Op. 42 ...	5	0

Twelve Part-songs for Medium Voice and Pianoforte, with explanatory text.

1. The tiny little house.
2. Dear lady Snow.
3. The little Bee.
4. Baby's Bedtime.
5. The Mice's Revenge.
6. Baby's Ride.
7. Playing at Trains.
8. The Visit!
9. The Omelette.
10. The good little girl's reply.
11. Skipping.
12. The story of Johnny

No.		s.	d.
823.	Ten Children-Scenes. Op. 54	5	0

With explanatory text.

1. Shuttlecocks.
2. The little scatterbrain.
3. Grandpapa.
4. The good Housekeeper.
5. The Oracle.
6. Tommy's got the sulks.
7. The sad story of the vain Duckling.
8. Cruel Anna.
9. The two Gossips.
10. When I've finished growing.

No.		s.	d.
988.	Six New Songs with action, for the very little ones. Op. 58	5	0

With explanatory text. (Callisthenic Studies.)

1. The little dumb maiden (Study in hand-movements).
2. Pit-a-Pat (Study in step-marching).
3. The pretty Doll (Study in expression: head and eyes).
4. Clever hands and fingers (Song with action).
5. Faithful little legs (Song with action).
6. The quick Dressmaker (Song with action).

No.		s.	d.
1010.	Ten Callisthenic Songs for young girls. Op. 60 ...	5	0

With explanatory text.

1. The white Maidens (Song with action).
2. The Statues (Song with action).
3. Clever hands and fingers (Song with action).
4. The Pedlar (Song with actions).
5. Faithful little Legs (Song with action).
6. The old Arm-chair (Song in three Pictures).
7. The two Dancing-Lessons (Song with action).
8. The golden-haired Fairy (Song with dance).
9. On a Sunday Morn (Marching exercise).
10. The quick Dressmaker.

FOUR UNISON SONGS IN BOTH NOTATIONS (Novello's School Music Review).

No.		s.	d.
*265.	Playfellows	0	2
*257.	The weaver's shuttle	0	2
*258.	The little worker	0	2
*262.	The circus (Junior unison song)	0	2

PIANOFORTE WORKS COMPOSED SPECIALLY FOR THE DEVELOPMENT OF PLASTIC INTERPRETATION.

No.		s.	d.
	*Quatre danses caractéristiques ...	4	0
411.	Six danses romandes. Op. 32 ...	3	6
412.	Six petites pièces. Op. 59 ...	2	6
578.	Six bagatelles. Op. 67 ...	2	6
780.	Marches rythmiques	4	6
1528.	Esquisses rythmiques	7	0

LONDON: NOVELLO AND COMPANY, LIMITED.
Sole Agents for Great Britain and the Colonies, and the United States of America, for most of the JAQUES-DALCROZE Publications, issued by JOBIN ET CIE., Lausanne.

RHYTHMIC MOVEMENT

VOL. II.

Bars of Six to Nine Beats
with a chapter on the application of Rhythmic
Movement to Pianoforte Technique.

BY

ÉMILE JAQUES-DALCROZE.

1921

LONDON: NOVELLO AND COMPANY, LIMITED.
NEW YORK: THE H. W. GRAY CO., SOLE AGENTS FOR THE U.S.A.
LAUSANNE: JOBIN & CIE.

THE JAQUES-DALCROZE

METHOD OF EURHYTHMICS.

HYTHMIC MOVEMENT

VOL. II.

Bars of Six to Nine Beats
with a chapter on the application of Rhythmic
Movement to Pianoforte Technique.

BY

ÉMILE JAQUES-DALCROZE.

1921

London: NOVELLO AND COMPANY, Limited.
New York: THE H. W. GRAY CO., Sole Agents for the U.S.A.
Lausanne: JOBIN & Cie.

MADE IN ENGLAND.

INDEX.

CHAPTER V.

SEXTUPLE TIME.

EXERCISES IN WALKING WHILE BEATING TIME.

PREPARATORY EXERCISE.

From beat	1	to beat	2.	Cross the arms over the chest.
,,	2	,,	3.	Extend them in front horizontally.
,,	3	,,	4.	Raise the hands till they are at right-angles with the forearm.
,,	4	,,	5.	Extend the arms sideways.
,,	5	,,	6.	Raise them vertically.
,,	6	,,	1.	Lower them energetically with an accent on one.

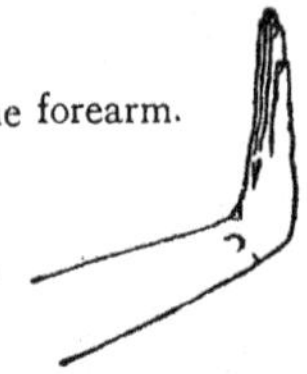

A bar of $\frac{6}{4}$ can be thought of as a slow bar of duple-time with a secondary accent on e fourth beat. While one arm beats six beats the other can beat two beats, thus:—

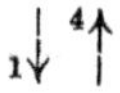

(a)  (b) with quavers 

(c) with 

(*d*) with syncopation  or  etc.

2. 

Repeat these exercises with all the anacrusic forms of $\frac{6}{4}$.

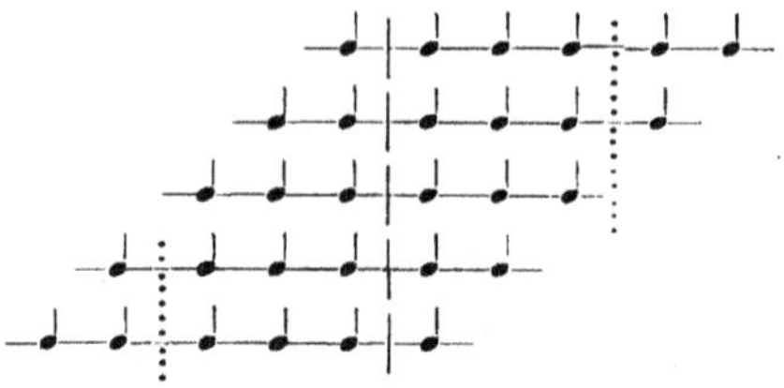

The same with quavers and semiquavers.

PHRASES AND RESTS.

PHRASING WITH THE ARMS AND FEET.

1. The arms beat
The feet step

etc.

WITH OTHER WAYS OF PHRASING.

2. 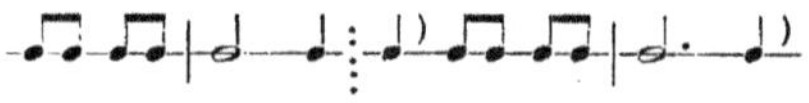 3. 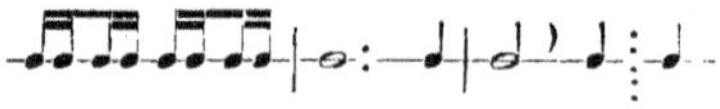

4. Phrases formed by variation of the secondary accent (each bar being of the same length).

See p. 4, bars of 6 pulse-units.

(*a*) 

(*b*) 

(*c*) 

See p. 4, bars of 12 pulse-units.

Phrasing by variation of the primary accent (each phrase being of the same length).

(**a**) 

ANALYSIS OF NOTE-VALUES.

Six times and one-sixth values.

The Note Sign $\frac{6}{4}$ 𝅝.

Execution.—1. Step. 2. Cross the free leg (bending the knee of supporting leg). 3. Extend the free leg in front. 4. Straighten the supporting leg, keeping the free leg extended in front. 5. Extend the free leg to one side. 6. Bring the free leg back to the supporting leg.

The note value 18/8 𝅜 :

Same execution as for 𝅝.

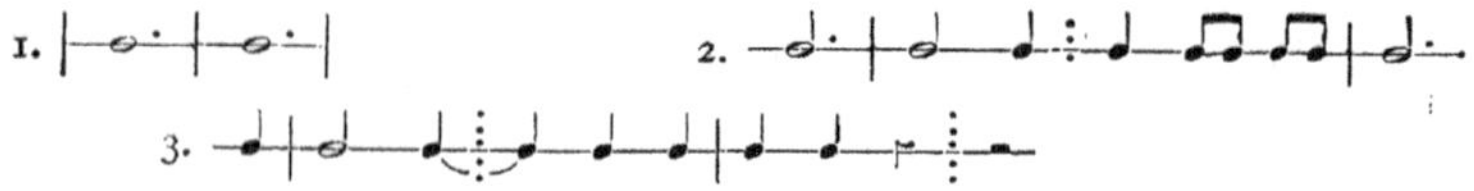

BARS OF 6 PULSE-UNITS.

The bar in $\frac{3}{2}$ is also composed of 6 crotchets, but with two secondary accents.

 One arm beats 3, the other 6.

BARS OF 12 PULSE-UNITS.

From 12 quavers or 12 semiquavers a bar can be formed either of 2 beats, of 3 beats, or of 4 beats.

12 ♪ forming a bar of 2 beats.

 One arm beats 6/4, the other 2/𝅗𝅥.

12 ♪ forming a bar of 3 beats.

 One arm beats 6/4, the other 3/2.

12 ♪ forming a bar of 4 beats.

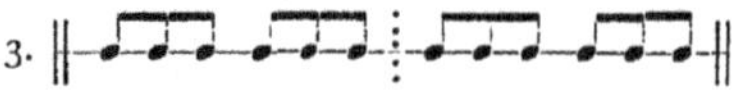 One arm beats 2/𝅗𝅥., the other 4/♩.

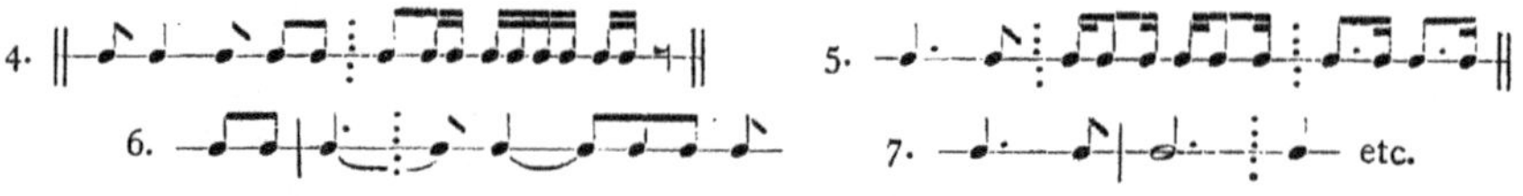

BARS OF 18 PULSE-UNITS.

18 quavers (or semiquavers) making a bar of 3 beats.

See p. 45, Nonuple time.

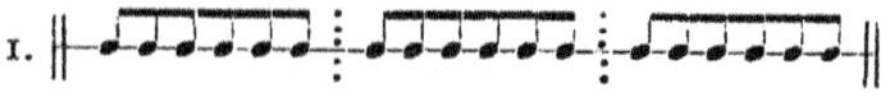

One arm beats 6/♩., the other arm 3/𝅗𝅥.

Anacrusic forms:

2. 

3.  etc., etc.

SYNCOPATION.

1. The pupils walk 6 steps to the bar, clapping in syncopation.

(*a*) feet
hands 

At *hopp* clap the beats, walk the syncopation.

(*b*) feet
hands 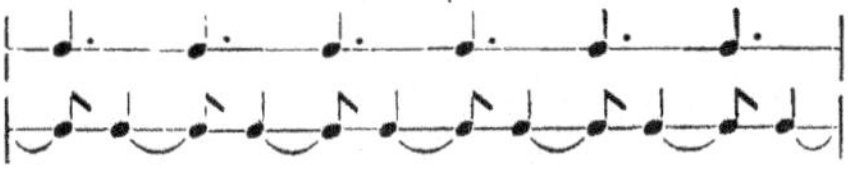

(*c*) feet
hands 

2. The same as 1, but at *hopp* feet and hands move twice or three times as fast or as slow.

3. The pupils walk  following the teacher's accelerando.

4. The pupils walk  accentuating the syncopation by breathing.

UNEQUAL BARS.

Examples of the same group of notes with varying accents.

 6/4 and 3/2

1. 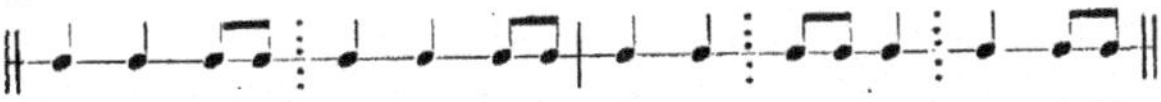 etc.

2.  etc.

18  forming bars of 2 and 3 beats

3. 

4. 

$\frac{6}{4}$ and $\frac{12}{8}$

5.
6.
7.

$\frac{3}{2}$ and $\frac{12}{8}$

8.
9.

MORE DIFFICULT EXERCISE.

10.
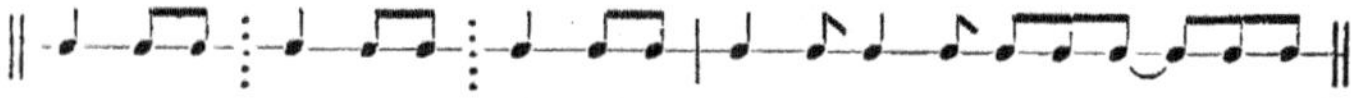

PLASTIC COUNTERPOINT.

Themes:

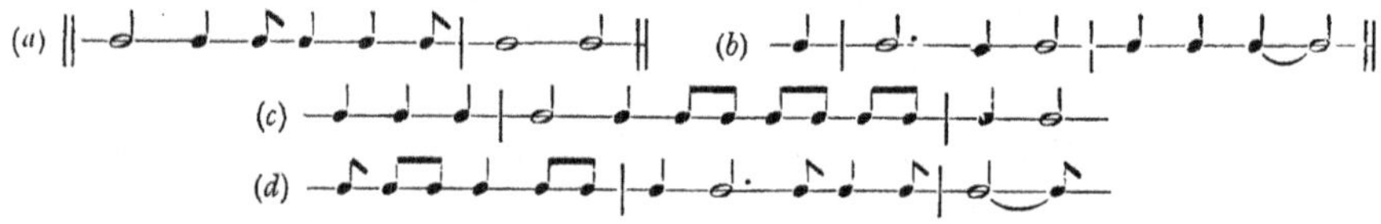

Realise the counterpoint of these themes:—the 1st time in ♩; the 2nd time in ♪; the 3rd time in 𝅘𝅥𝅯.

The counterpoint to be realised, the 1st time in ♪; the 2nd time in 𝅘𝅥𝅯

BREATHING.

Use only those rhythms which are suitable for breathing exercises.

e.g.:
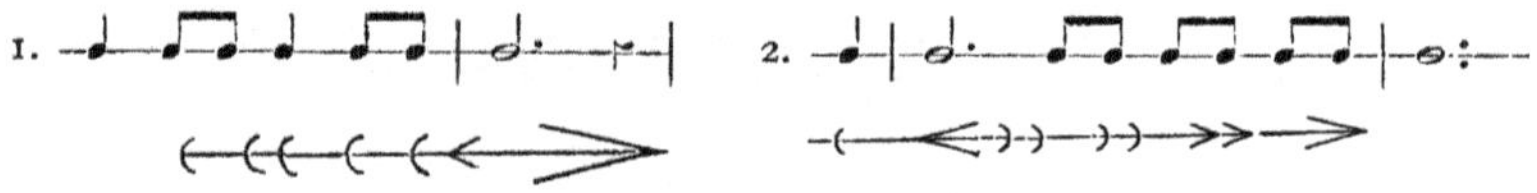

3. The pupils form a compact group, body relaxed with no contraction whatsoever, both hands clasped in front.

(*a*) Raise the hands to waist-level, breathe in 

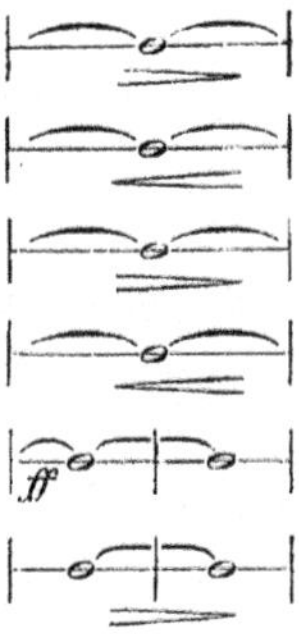

(*b*) Breathe out, keeping the ribs raised.

(*c*) Raise the hands to shoulder-level, breathe in.

(*d*) Breathe out, keeping the ribs raised.

(*e*) Raise the arms obliquely. Breathe in, bending the body forward, in preparation for a step.

(*f*) Make an accented step, and keep the weight of the body on the supporting leg, while singing a given note *ff* for 2 bars.

(*g*) Continue singing but with *decrescendo*, gradually relaxing the body.

INDEPENDENCE OF THE LIMBS.

FIRST PREPARATORY EXERCISE.

(*a*) Make the movements 1 to 9 then 9 to 1 with one arm according to the scheme below.

(*b*) The same with both arms.

N.B.—Movements which cover a large area will be executed more rapidly than those covering a smaller area, although the time taken for the movements is the same.

See *lengths of step* and *of spacing*, Vol. I., pp. 9, 12, and 13.

Exercise 1. One arm beats through an increasing area (1-2 to 1-9), whilst the other arm beats through a decreasing area (1-9 to 1-2), in the same length of time.

LINES OF MOVEMENT FOR EXERCISE 1.

(*a*) In the same direction.

(*b*) In opposite directions.

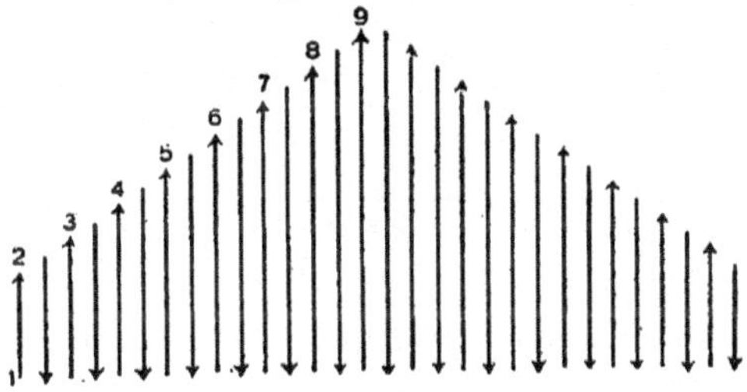

2ND PREPARATORY EXERCISE.

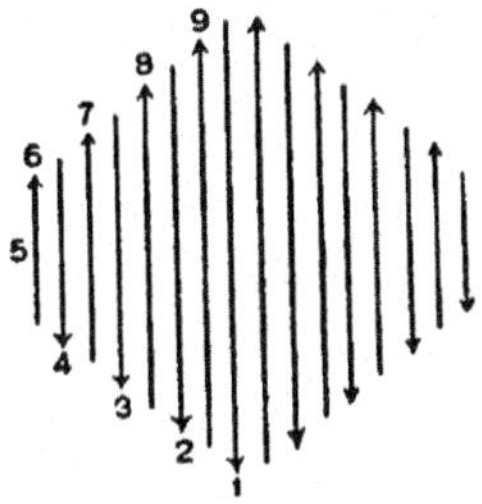

(*a.*) With one arm.

(*b.*) With both arms.

3RD PREPARATORY EXERCISE.

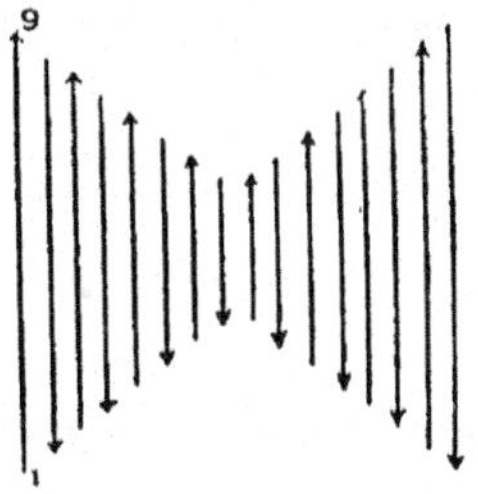

(*a.*) With one arm.

(*b.*) With both arms.

Exercise 2. One arm makes movements forming a crescendo followed by a diminuendo (5-6 to 1-9); the other arm doing the opposite (1-9 to 5-6) and *vice-versa,* in the same length of time. (*a*) In the same direction, (*b*) in opposite directions.

DIAGRAM OF THE LINES OF MOVEMENT MADE BY THE TWO ARMS.

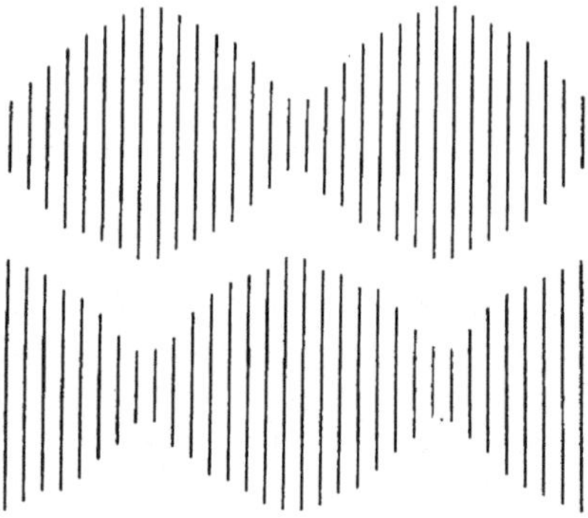

CONTROL AND INHIBITION.

1. The pupil walks quavers, at *hopp* ♩. ♪

e.g.:

etc.

The rhythms are to be remembered and then realised without *hopp.*

2. The pupil walks ♩. ♪ at *hopp* quavers

etc.

Comparison of ♩. ♪ ♫ with ♩. ♪♪♪

3. The pupil walks $\frac{6}{8}$ ♩. ♪♪♪, at *hopp* the same rhythm $\frac{3}{4}$ ♩. ♪ ♫

4. The pupil walks the anacrusic forms of $\frac{6}{4}$. At *hopp* twice as fast. At the 2nd *hopp* the original tempo. At the 3rd *hopp* twice as slow. At the 4th *hopp* the original tempo.

e.g.: (*a*)
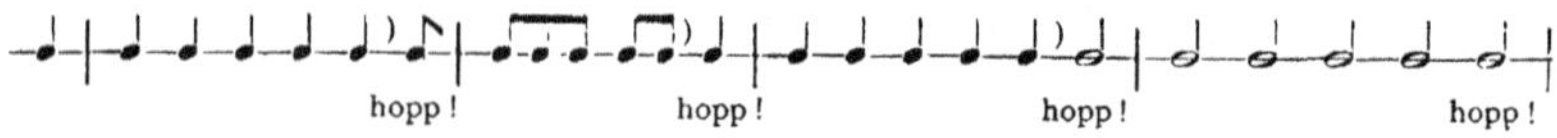

(*b*) 

The same with the remaining anacrusic forms.

5. Repeat exercise 3 three times as fast and as slow.

6. The pupil walks , at *hopp* once.

7. The pupil walks When the teacher calls *two, three, four, five, six*, or *seven*, that number of steps is inserted on the beat following the command.

Example 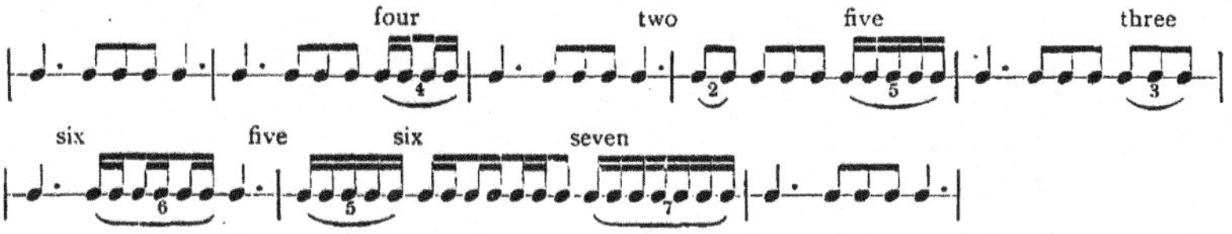

When this exercise has been repeated several times the pupil realises it without *hopp*.

AURAL EXERCISES.

1. The pupils clap throughout in syncopation The teacher plays a sequence of bars which the pupils realise with the feet one bar later. (This kind of canon is also called "continuous realisation.")

2. The teacher plays the scale of C, and points out that there are semitones between E and F and between B and C.

Then he plays (or sings) sequences of tones and semitones. When he plays a tone the pupils walk the following bar, taking large steps; when he plays a semitone the pupils walk the following bar, taking small steps:—

Example: 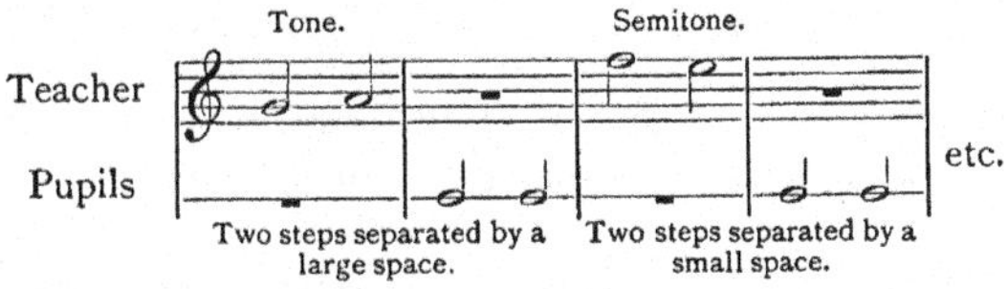

N.B.—This exercise can also be done on a staircase (two steps on the same stair for the two notes after a semitone).

N.B.—The pupils write down the rhythms studied during the lesson.

DIVISION OF A NOTE INTO SHORTER VALUES.

1. Teacher
Pupil

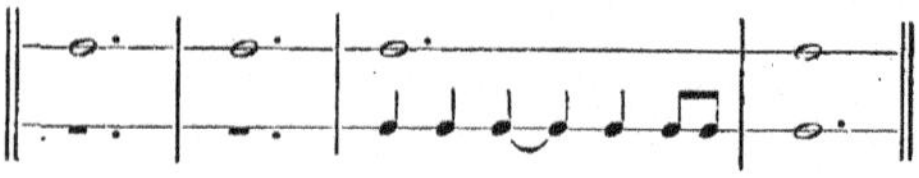

2. Teacher
Pupil

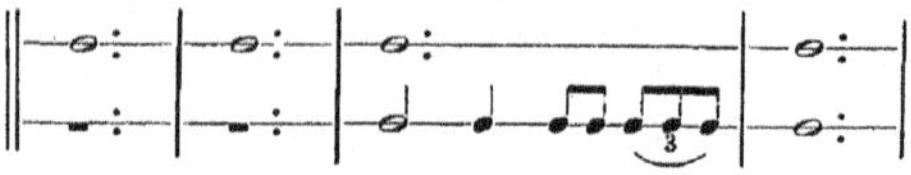

3. Teacher
Pupil

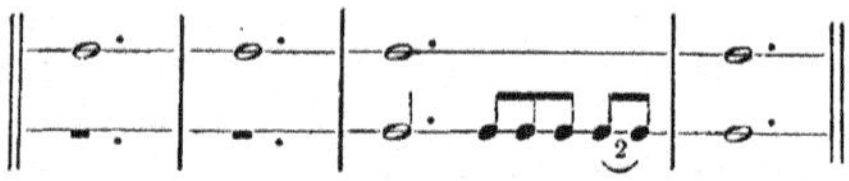

First time *adagio;* second time *allegretto;* third time *moderato,* etc.

As can be seen above, the teacher plays two long notes and at the third bar the pupils realise a given theme in the time of this note.

IMPROVISATION.

1. A pupil improvises a theme of two bars, and the class then walks the counterpoint.

2. A pupil improvises a theme of two bars. Another pupil immediately walks the counterpoint to this two-bar theme, and then improvises two new bars; to which the first pupil walks the counterpoint, etc.

1st pupil
2nd pupil

etc.

3. Two pupils are chosen as soloists. The first improvises one bar, the second immediately adds another bar. This sequence of two bars is repeated several times, and at *Hopp!* the rest of the pupils realise the counterpoint of the two bars.

4. A pupil realises by means of large or small steps the succession of tones and semitones characteristic of a given scale. The class must find out what scale is intended.

EXERCISES IN CONDUCTING.

A pupil conducts: 1. With accelerando and ritardando.

2. With piano, forte, decrescendo, crescendo.

3. Bars composed of the same notes with varying secondary accents.

(*a*)  and 

(*b*)  and 

(*c*)  considered as a bar of 3 ♩

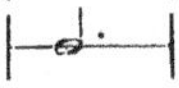 considered as a bar of $\frac{6}{8}$

(*d*) 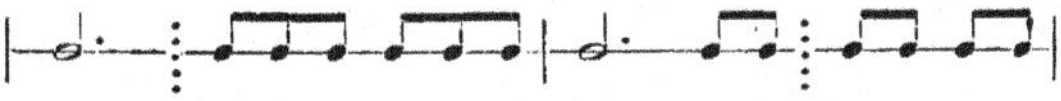 etc.

FREE EXERCISES.

For three groups.

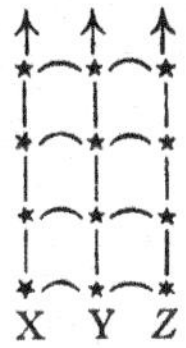

The pupils stand side by side in 3 files. Each group of three hold hands.

On 1st beat swinging movement of arms and body backward } two bars.
On 2nd beat swinging movement of arms and body forward }

On the 1st beat of the 3rd bar swing back again.

On the 2nd beat of the 3rd bar the line Y runs forward as if impelled by swinging movements of X and Z. These latter remain on the spot.

On the 2nd beat of the 5th bar the lines X and Z skip forward. The line Y stands still, looking back towards X and Z and stretching out hands to them.

On 1 of the 8th bar the pupils take hands and begin again.

In a circle or spiral.

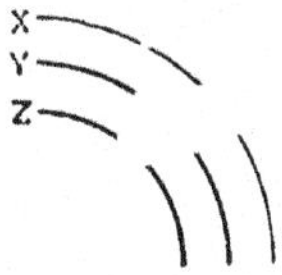

Bars 1 to 3.

Bars 3 to 5.

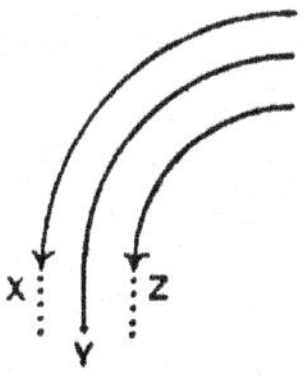

Bars 5 to 7.

*Marches Rythmiques,** Nos. 23 to 26, and *Esquisses Rythmiques,* No. 5.

* Lausanne: JOBIN ET CIE. London: NOVELLO & Co., Ltd., 160, Wardour Street, W.1.

CHAPTER VI.

SEPTUPLE TIME.

EXERCISES IN MARCHING WHILE BEATING TIME.

Preparatory Exercise.

From beat 1 to beat 4.	As in $\frac{6}{4}$.
„ „ 4 „ „ 5.	Again cross the arms over the chest.
„ „ 5 „ „ 7.	The same movements as from 4 to 6 in $\frac{6}{4}$.
Then to 1.	As in $\frac{6}{4}$.

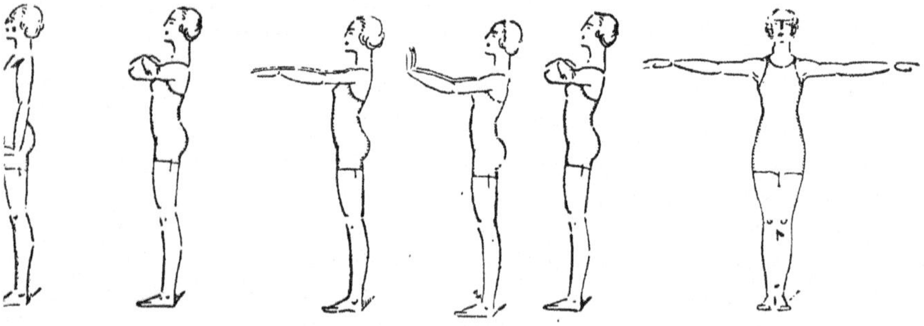

1. (a) 

(b) with quavers.

(c) with semiquavers.

} and all the anacrusic forms.

2. 

Secondary Accents.

3. (a) (b) (c)

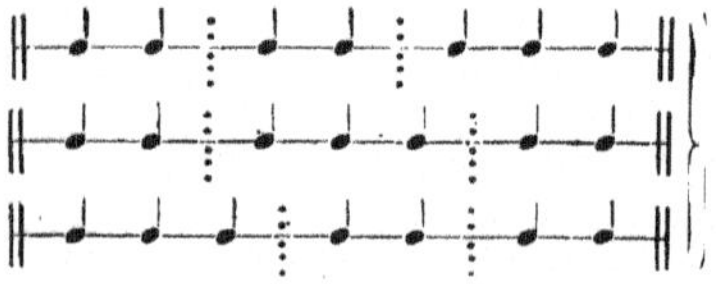

One arm beats $\frac{7}{4}$. The other arm beats 3 unequal beats according to the position of the secondary accents.

MORE DIFFICULT EXERCISES.

4. (a) (b) (c) (d) (e)

PHRASES AND RESTS.

1. 2. 3. 4.

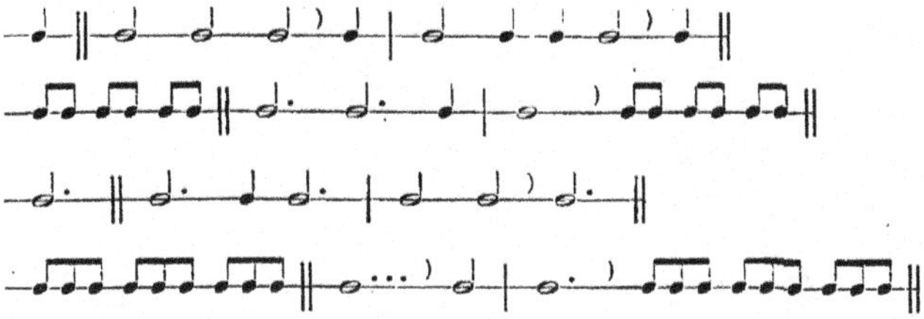

etc.

See p. 16, Vol. I.

CÆSURA.

5. The cæsura (or period of rest separating two phrases or two periods) may be made by a bar executed three times as fast or as slow.

(a) (b) (c) (d) (e)

The sign ÷ means that the preceding bar or rhythm is to be repeated.

ANALYSIS OF NOTE VALUES

Seven times and one-seventh values.

The note sign $\frac{7}{4}$ o ..

Execution : 1, 2, 3, 4 : as in the note of six beats.
5 : the free leg is extended behind, the supporting leg is bent.
6, 7 : as 5 and 6 in o˙.

$\frac{21}{8}$ |o| ::

Same execution as for o ..

EXERCISES.

BARS OF 14 NOTES.

14 quavers forming a bar in 2 time.

Other groupings:

♪ = ♪ 14 ♪ forming a bar in 4 time.

14 ♪ forming a bar in 5 time.

14 ♪ forming a bar in 6 time.

The same with rhythms:

UNEQUAL BARS.

(*a*) Formed by means of secondary accents.
(*b*) Formed by adding or dropping a beat.

♩ = ♩ $\frac{7}{4}$

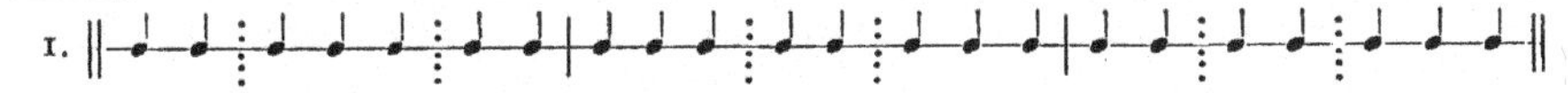

𝅗𝅥 : = 𝅗𝅥 : $\frac{14}{8}$ and $\frac{21}{8}$

♪ = ♪ $\frac{7}{4}$ or $\frac{14}{8}$

BARS OF 21 PULSE-UNITS.

7/♩. and 3/𝅗𝅥..

etc.

More difficult exercises. The preceding exercises, with the addition of rhythms. *E.g.*, each bar is of the same length, the pupil does not subdivide the long notes except in the case of syncopation.

6. 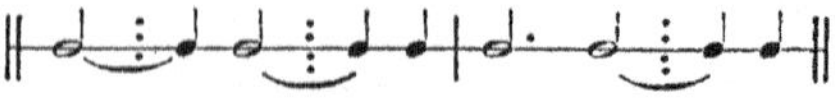

7. 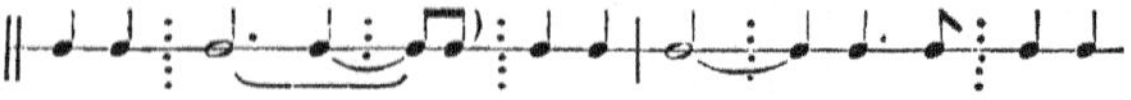

SPRINGS.

1. 

2. 

etc.

3. 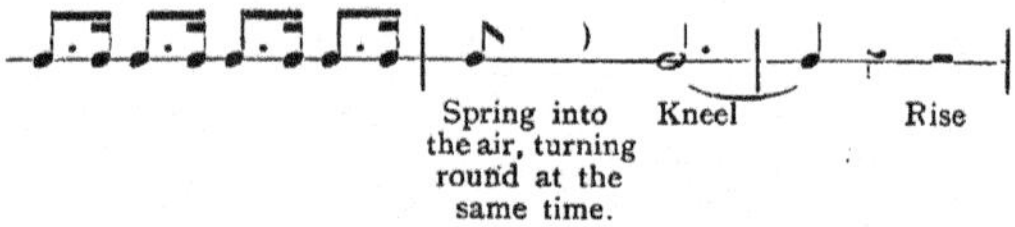

RESTS.

Rests may be caused by:

1. Fatigue.
2. The necessity for preparing an accent or the resumption of a theme.

The two may be combined.

Examples:

(a) 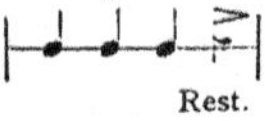

Here the preparation for the next bar is made only at the last moment of the 4th beat. The cessation of movement caused by fatigue.

(b) 

Here the 3 minims are of equal strength. The relaxation is made abruptly on the 7th beat, the preparation for the next bar begins on the 8th beat.

(c) 

In this case the relaxation begins on the 6th beat during the bend. The preparation during the 7th and 8th beats.

(d) 

Here the preparation which begins on the 7th beat is interrupted on the 8th beat by a fresh access of fatigue.

(Use breathing. Study these rests also in exercises *for separate limbs*, etc.)

ANACRUSIC FORMS TO BE USED FOR TWICE AS FAST AND TWICE AS SLOW.

1. 

2. 

BREATHING.

(See Vol. I., pp. 18 and 19.)

Use only those rhythms which can easily be interpreted by breathing.

E.g.:

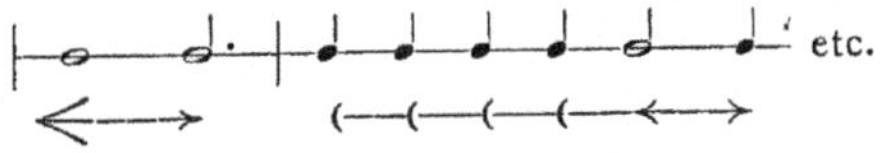

Singing Exercise.—Take a deep and slow inspiration, then clench the fists and contract the whole body from the feet upwards, pressing the soles of the feet firmly on the ground, then sing any note and control the sound with a strong feeling of muscular resistance, economising the breath.

Another Exercise.—Breathe in as in the preceding exercise, then sing a note *ff*. From time to time the body relaxes (diminution of contraction) and the voice follows it.

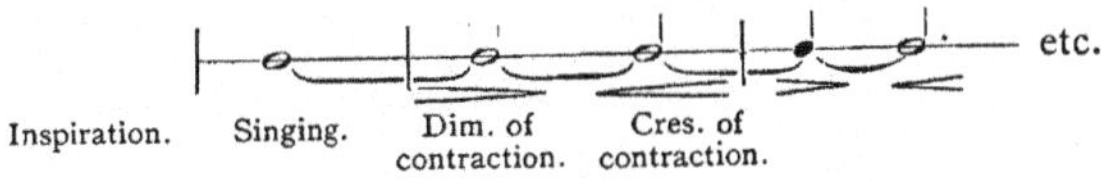

N.B.—The lines in the 2nd and 3rd bars are signs of dynamic variation, not of breathing.

INDEPENDENCE OF LIMBS.

1. Clap

Mark time with the feet

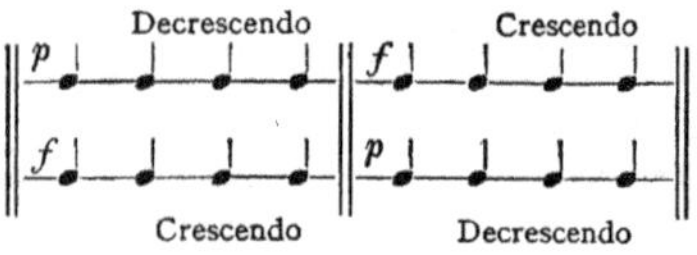

2. Arms

Feet (mark time)

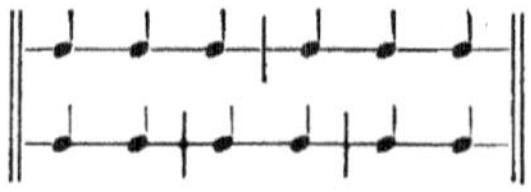

3. Arms

Feet (mark time)

When the arm and foot movements coincide on the metric accent, make a spring.

N.B.—These can also be realised by the arms using the gestures for beating time. If the rhythm to be realised contains 5 notes, the gestures for 5 time are used, etc.

Themes to be realised by the arms:

(*a*) 

(*b*) 

(*c*) 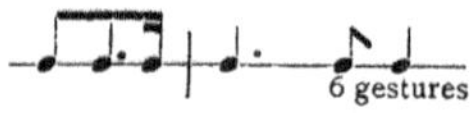

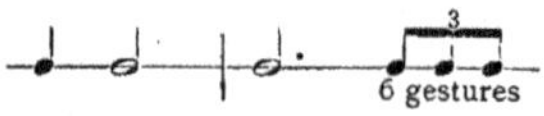

Repeat changing arms. The feet walk 

Themes to realise.—One note with the foot, the following note by a gesture of the arms or by clapping.

1.  2.  3. 

4. 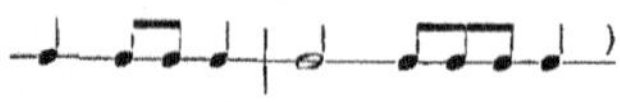 5. 

CONTROL.

1. Head-bending; clapping; stamping at the word of command.

etc.

2. March, beating time. At *hopp*, lie down, continue counting mentally. At *hopp*, rise, beat time, and walk.

3. at *hopp*, spring to the side.

4. At command: *Two* once.
" " *Three* "
" " *Four* "
" " *Hopp*, skip once.

5. One pupil conducts. The other pupils walk with arms extended outwards. When the conductor marks a pathetic accent on any beat, the other pupils make one skip.

E.g.:  etc.

6. At *hopp*, 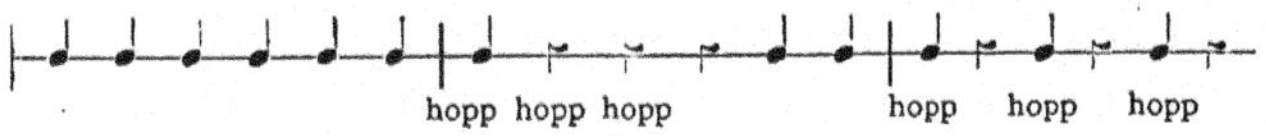

etc.

The same exercise backward.

7. The teacher gives the pupils, who are standing in line, a rhythm to realise with steps and a gesture (or 2 gestures).

E.g.:

Feet
Gesture

etc.

The teacher plays 3 bars expressive of a certain mood and tempo; at the 4th bar realise the rhythm in the given mood and tempo.

EXERCISES IN HEARING.

1. The teacher plays 𝅝. At the 3rd 𝅝. the pupils walk a given rhythm, *e.g.*, in the time of the 𝅝.

2. Counterpoint, with breathing on the 2nd half of each note.

Feet . . . . .
Counterpoint with breathing

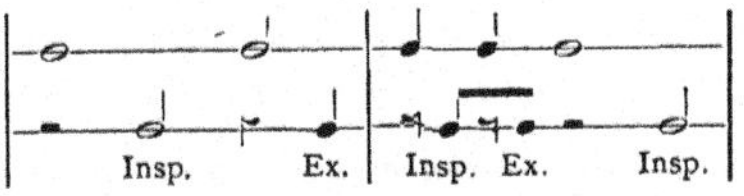

etc.

N.B.—Movements of the trunk can be used instead of breathing.

3. Counterpoint in , *e.g.:*

 etc.

N.B.—The theme may be realised with gestures whilst the counterpoint is realised by the feet.

4. The pupils write down the rhythms they have heard.

5. The pupils realise some of the rhythms formed of unequal bars given at the end of this volume.

IMPROVISATION.

Variations.—1. A pupil improvises an anacrusic theme; a second pupil repeats it with a slight variation; a third pupil repeats it with another variation.

E.g.:  etc.

2. A pupil invents a rhythm, in which the group  occurs once.

E.g.:  the class repeats the theme.

3. A pupil improvises one or two bars with *pathetic accents.*

4. A pupil improvises a simple bar which he repeats, singing the notes of the scale of C.

5. Free improvisation, walking and singing at the same time.

INTERPRETATION OF GIVEN THEMES BY MEANS OF THE LEG MOVEMENTS OF THE LONGER NOTE VALUES.

All rhythms involving not more than nine notes can be realised by the leg movements which are used to divide 

E.g.: The theme  can be realised by the three leg-movements of the 

The theme  by the five leg-movements of the 

The theme  by the seven leg-movements of the 

INTERPRETATION OF GIVEN THEMES BY ALTERNATE MOVEMENTS OF THE ARMS, TRUNK, HEAD, AND LEGS.

E.g.: 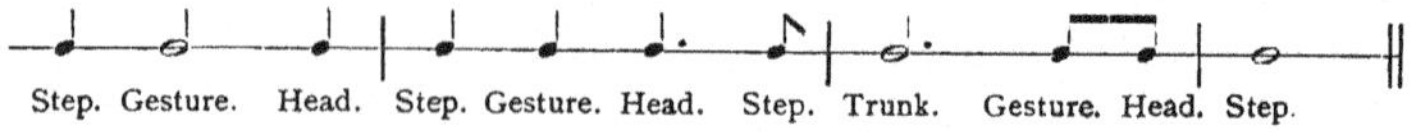

Or again the teacher can arrange beforehand a series of gestures and attitudes by which the pupils can realise a given theme.

ANALYSIS OF SLOW MOVEMENTS.

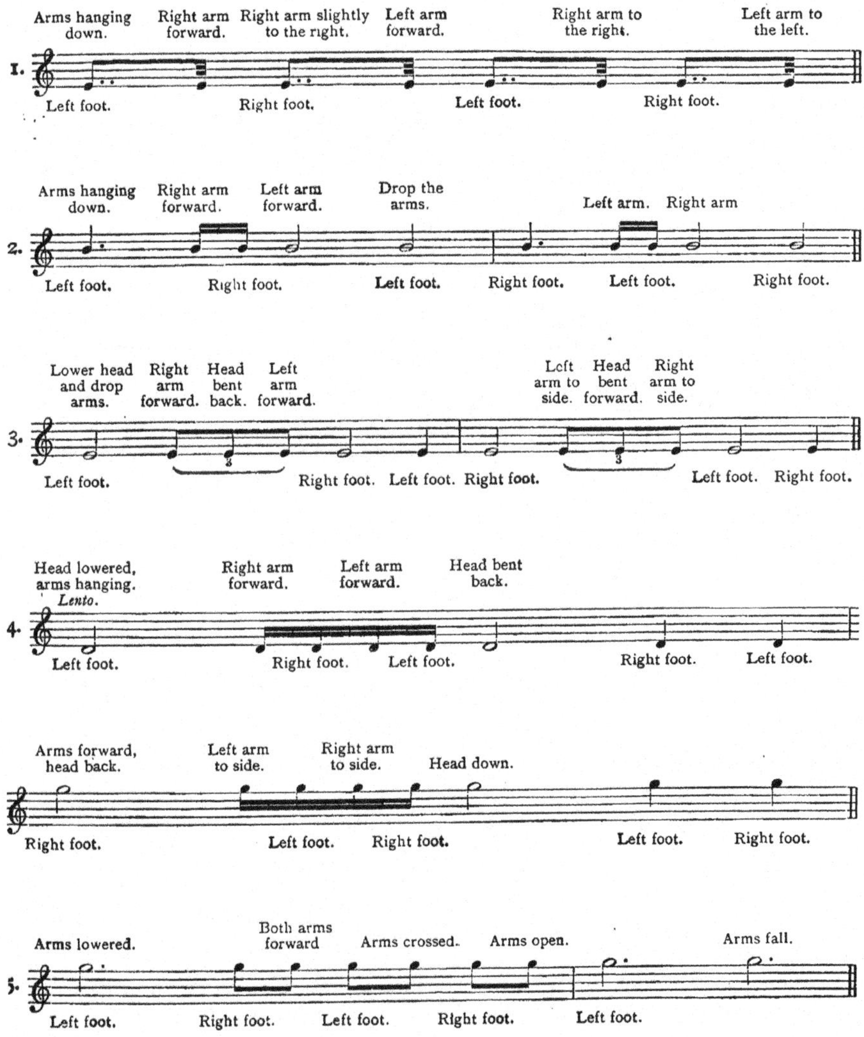

EXERCISES IN CONDUCTING.

1. A pupil conducts with accelerando, ritardando, crescendo, and decrescendo.

2. A pupil conducts with movements of different length. The other pupils imitate the movements.

3. One pupil conducts a given theme, first one group then another responding to his conducting. The theme to be sung:

4. A pupil placed between two groups conducts in two-time for group 1, in three-time for group 2; he may change the bar-time at will.

ADDITIONAL EXERCISES.

1. The pupils are grouped at the far end of the hall. The teacher plays an accented rhythm such as  or , first pianissimo, then by slow crescendo to *ff*. The pupils begin by interpreting it with small movements of the wrist, then of the arms, and finally by swaying the whole body to and fro, till at the climax of *ff* the legs, impelled by the swing of the body, move with the rhythm.

2. *The scale.* Seven pupils realise fragments of the following theme one after the other:

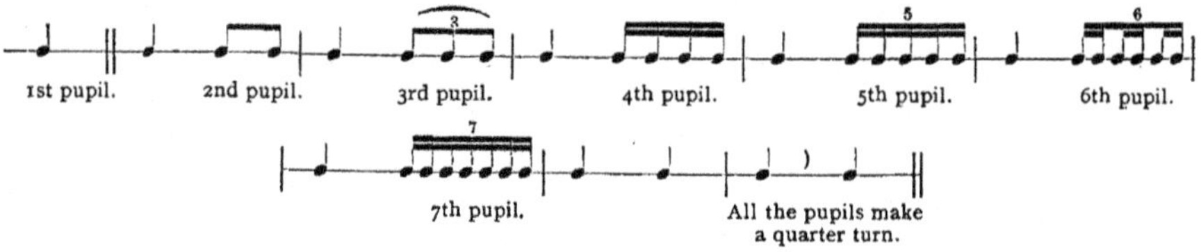

and the 7th pupil, now become the 1st, begins the exercise again. The remainder of the class sit on the ground and sing:

etc.

At the first repetition: 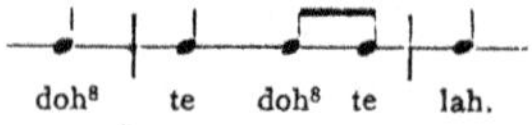

etc.

During the 1st, 3rd, 5th, and 7th execution of the given theme the pupils raise their arms, during the 2nd, 4th, 6th, and 8th execution they lower them so that after each execution they are alternately in oblique and straight lines. After 8 executions (*a-c*) they are at the starting-point.

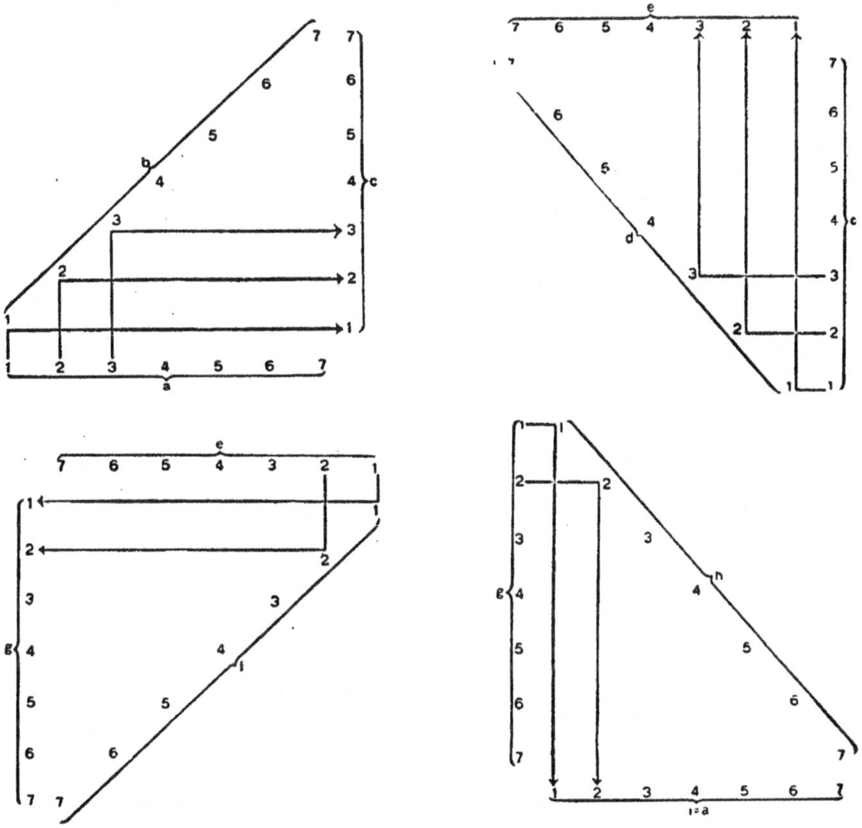

Canon in 4 parts for 8 pupils.

Fine.

Four couples stand one behind the other; they describe the following lines of movement (walking or running):

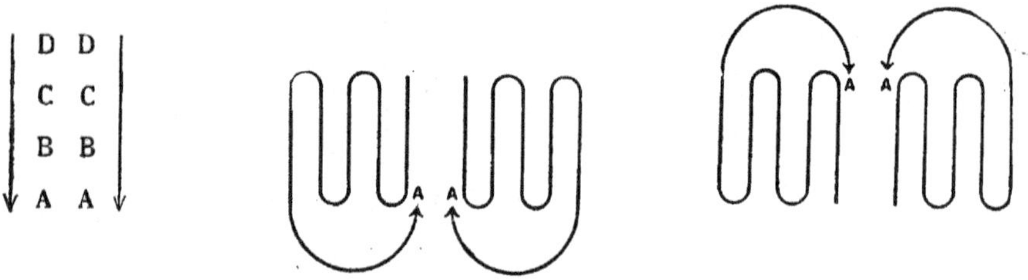

At the end of the first line of movement A begins the theme for the third time.

At the end of the second line, A A for the fourth time walks the three last steps ♩. ♩. ♩. of the theme.

The last step of the other parts coincides also with this last step of the A's.

N.B.—The manner of skipping to be chosen in advance.

See *Marches Rythmiques* Nos. 27 to 41 and *Exercices de Plastique animée* (Lausanne: Jobin et Cie; London: Novello & Co., Ltd.).

CHAPTER VII.

OCTUPLE TIME.

EXERCISES IN WALKING WHILE BEATING TIME.

PREPARATORY EXERCISE.

From beat 1 to beat 5. As in $\frac{7}{4}$.
,, ,, 5 ,, 6. The arms are extended in front on a level with the shoulders.
,, ,, 6 ,, 8. As in the beats 5 to 7 in $\frac{7}{4}$.

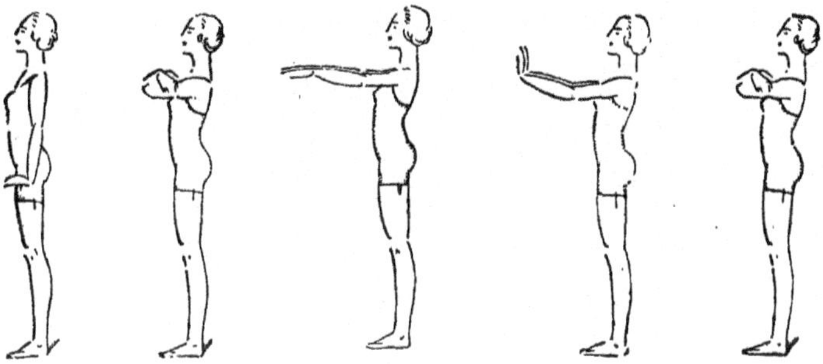

4. 5.

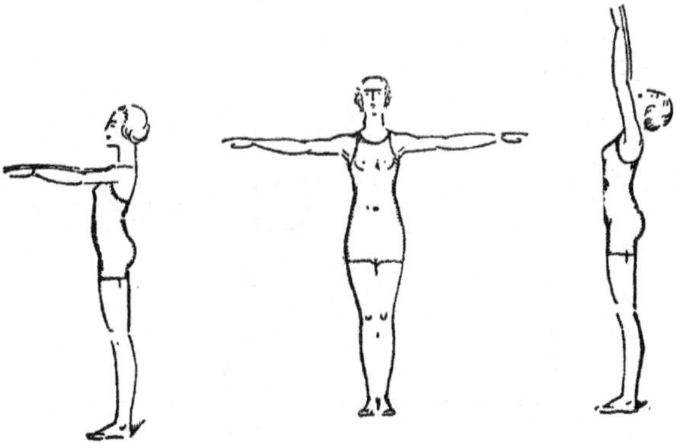

6.

1. (*a*)  (*b*) with quavers; (*c*) with semiquavers, also with all the anacrusic forms.

2. 

3. 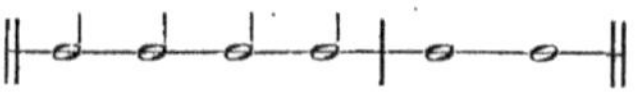 4. 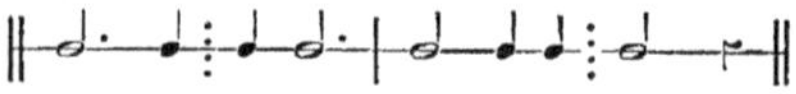

5.  etc., etc.

MORE DIFFICULT EXERCISES WITH SECONDARY ACCENTS.

(*a*) One arm beats $\frac{8}{4}$. The other beats $\frac{4}{2}$.

(*b*) One arm beats $\frac{8}{4}$. The other beats $\frac{2}{1}$.*

6. 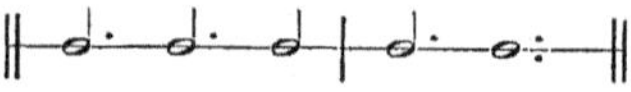 7. 

PERIODS AND RESTS.

1. Arms: Right arm.

Left arm.

Feet.

2. Head (Up-down).

Clap: Left hand on right.

Right hand on left.

Skip.

3. Head (left to right & rt. to l.)

Clap: Left hand on right.

Right hand on left.

Run.

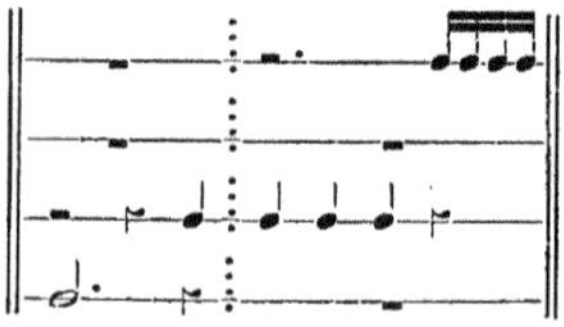

PERIODS AND PHRASES.

The Cæsura may consist of:

(*a*) A silent bar.
(*b*) A bar of quicker or slower movement.
(*c*) A bar two or three times as fast or as slow.
(*d*) A new bar containing a new rhythm.
(*e*) A change of rhythm.
(*f*) The repetition of the last bars.
(*g*) The repetition of the last motive.
(*h*) The interpretation of the end of a rhythm as the beginning of the next phrase.
(*i*) The repetition *and* development of the preceding phrase.
(*k*) One of the elements of the rhythm taken two or three times as slow.

EXAMPLES OF EIGHT-BAR PHRASES.

2×4=8. 4. 

5. 

4×2=8. 6. 

7. 

3+3+2=8. 8. 

2+3+3=8. 9. 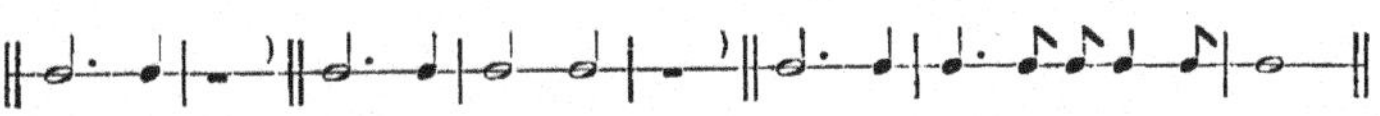

3+2+3=8. 10. 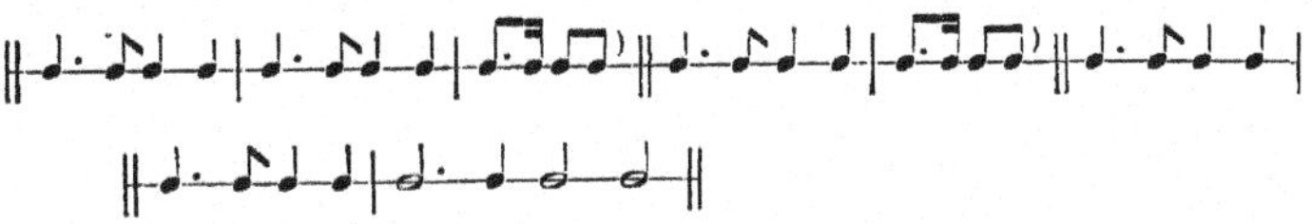

5+1+2=8. 11. 

2+6=8. 12. 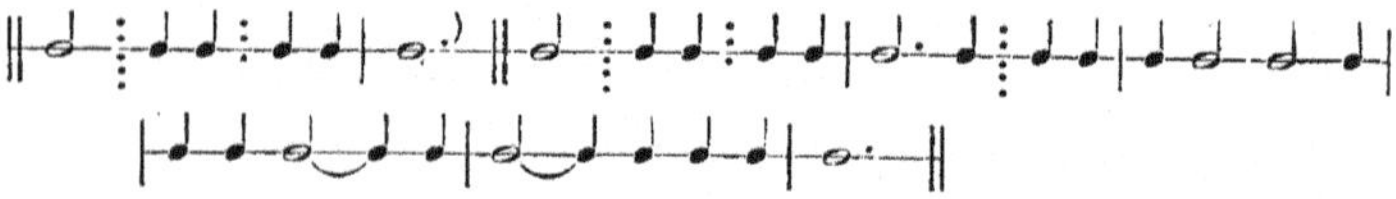

5+3=8. 13. 

3+5=8. 14. 

ANALYSIS OF NOTE-VALUES.

EIGHT TIMES AND ONE-EIGHTH VALUES.

The note of 8 beats

Execution: 1, 2, 3, 4, 5 as in the note of 7 beats.
6, cross the free leg behind, bend the supporting leg.
7, 8 as 6 and 7 in the note of 7 beats.

The note $\frac{24}{8}$ |𝅜|. Same execution as in the note of 7 beats.

1. 

2. 

3. 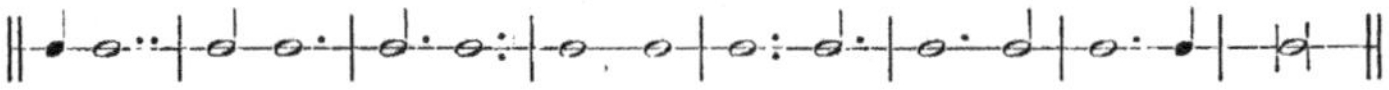

BARS COMPOSED OF TWENTY-FOUR PULSE-UNITS.

See *six and twelve*, page 4.

24 ♪ forming a bar of 8 beats.

♩. = ♩. 24/8 1. 

24 ♪ forming a bar of 6 beats.

𝅗𝅥 = 𝅗𝅥 6/2 2. 

24 ♪ forming a bar of 4 beats.

𝅗𝅥. = 𝅗𝅥. 12/4 3. 

24 ♪ forming a bar of 3 beats.

𝅝 = 𝅝 3/1 4. 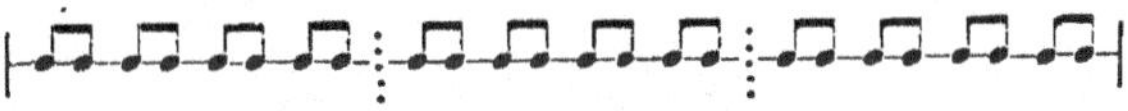

UNEQUAL BARS { Four bars in two-time. Two bars in four-time. One bar in eight-time.

♩ = ♩ 1. 

♩. = ♩. 2. From $\frac{3}{8}$ to $\frac{24}{8}$ and vice versâ.

 etc.

THE SAME WITH RHYTHMS.

E.g.: 3. 

4.  etc.

MORE DIFFICULT EXERCISES.

SEMIQUAVERS TAKEN TWICE AS FAST— DEMISEMIQUAVERS.

RHYTHMS TWICE AS FAST AND AS SLOW

(without subdivision of longer note-values).

WITH UNIFORMITY OF BAR.

(The arms do not participate in the change of time.)

The feet step the given rhythm:

Once in the original time Twice as fast Four times as fast Eight times as fast	in the same length of time.

4/2 1.

4/4 2.

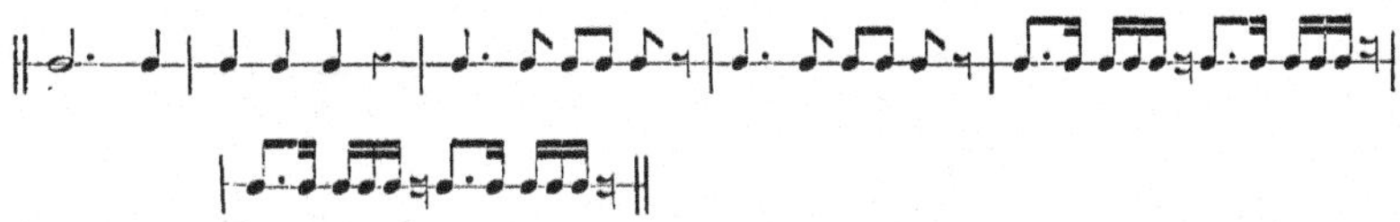

3.

WITH UNEQUAL BARS (More difficult exercises).
(The arms also change time.)

4.

5.

WITH ANACRUSIC THEMES (More difficult exercises).
(The arms take part in the change of time.)

The change of time begins with the anacrusis. An exceptional bar results.

PREPARATORY EXERCISES.

The arms beat 2/4 (a)

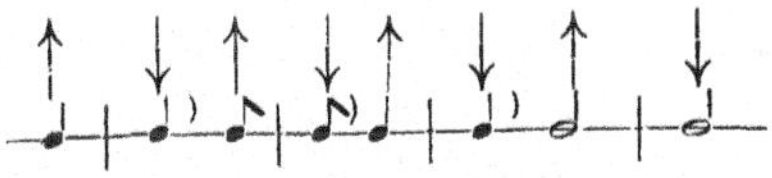

The arms beat 4/4 (b)

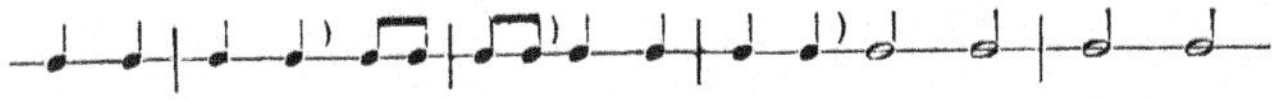

(c)

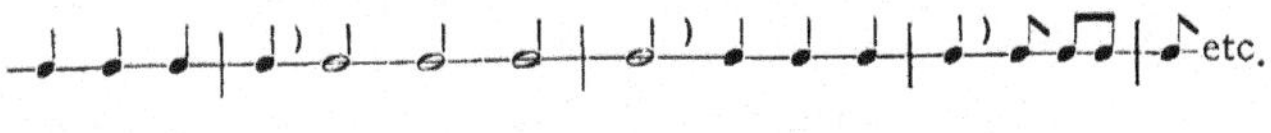

The arms beat 8/4

6.

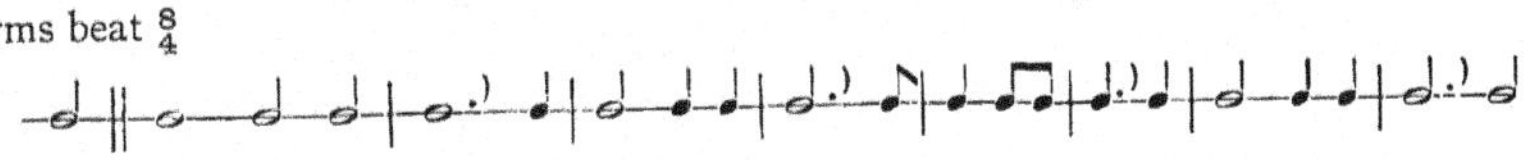

7.

SYNCOPATION WITH THE OCCASIONAL INTRODUCTION OF THE SAME TWICE AS FAST.

1. 

2. 

Lento.

3. 

4. 

Lento.

5. 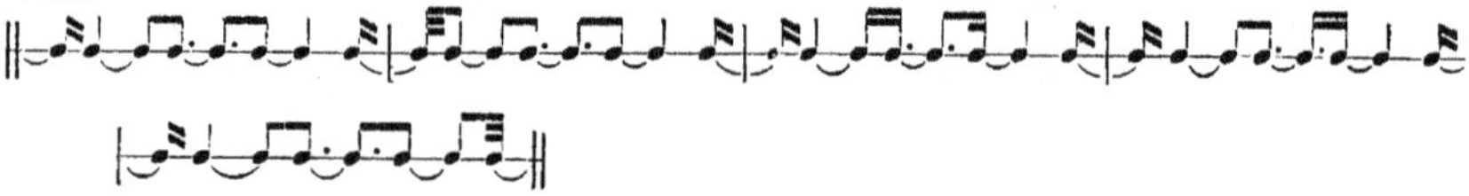

BREATHING.

1. Use the easiest of the new rhythms as breathing exercises:

Lento.

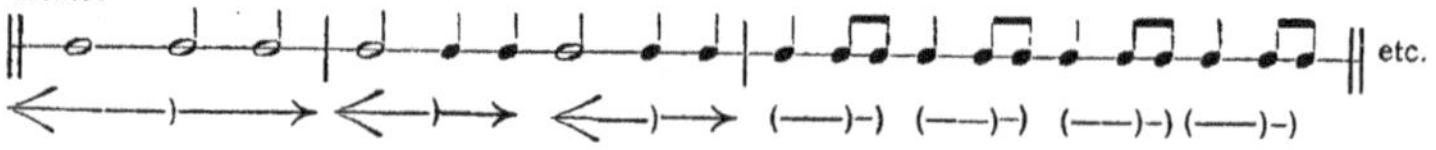

INFLUENCE OF BREATHING ON MOVEMENTS.

2. Kneel with bowed head; take a deep breath, at the same time raising the body in such a way as to suggest that it has been forced upward.

Before taking the breath the body should be entirely relaxed.

3. (*a*) The breathing now coincides with the raising of the thigh.
(*b*) ,, ,, ,, with raising one or both arms.
(*c*) ,, ,, ,, with straightening the bent trunk.
(*d*) ,, ,, ,, with making a step forward or backward.
(*e*) ,, ,, ,, with muscular expansion of the whole body.
(*f*) ,, ,, ,, with crossing or raising the arms.

4. The pupils skip for 2 bars. At the 3rd they pause in a prearranged position, taking breath; during the 4th bar they breathe out.

N.B.—During the expiration, the trunk may be turned to the right or the left, causing one lung to expand more than the other.

5. During the inspiration : imagine that a strong elastic band is held by its two ends. Then stretch this band, either with the two arms pulling in opposite directions, or with one arm fixed and the other pulling.

During the expiration : make movements that shall suggest relaxing the elastic.

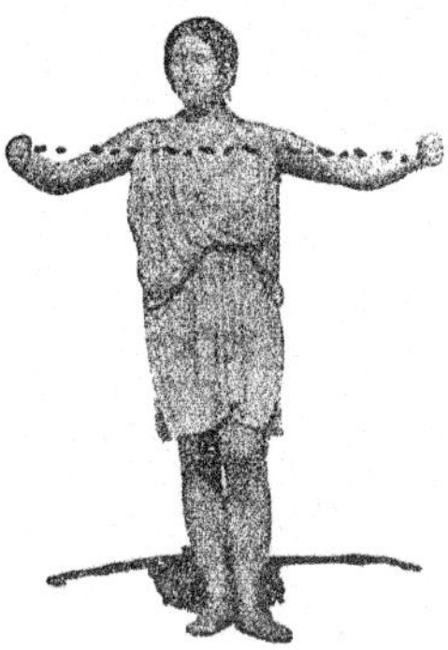

INDEPENDENCE OF LIMBS.

1. Bend and raise the head.

Clap.

Feet mark time.

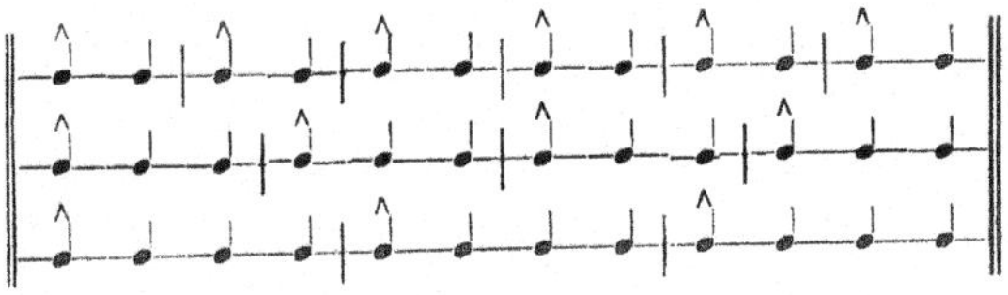

When all the accents coincide, make a spring.

2. Left arm.

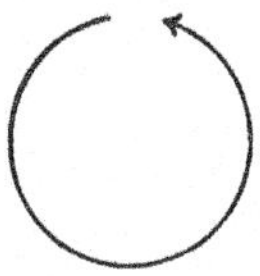

Right arm.

Feet mark time.

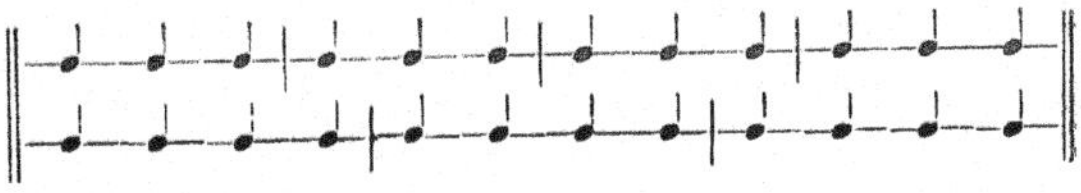

3. Increase of tension in one limb coincident with decrease of tension in another.

(*a*) Arm.

Thigh or calf.

Repeat, using right forearm and left hand, and vice versâ.

(*b*) Right arm.

Left arm.

Legs.

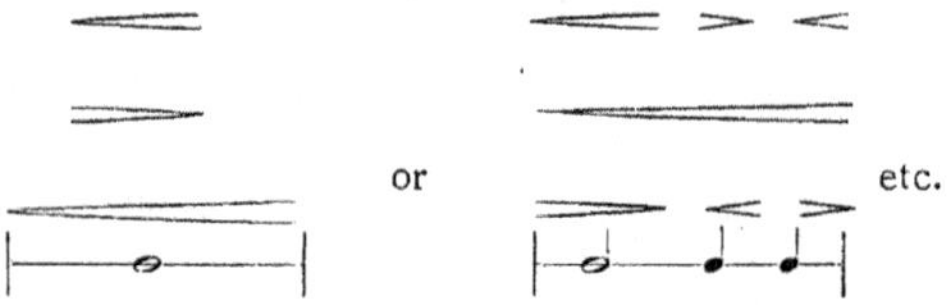

Repeat with other limbs, also with the diaphragm.

(*c*) Right arm.

Left arm.

Right leg.

Left leg.

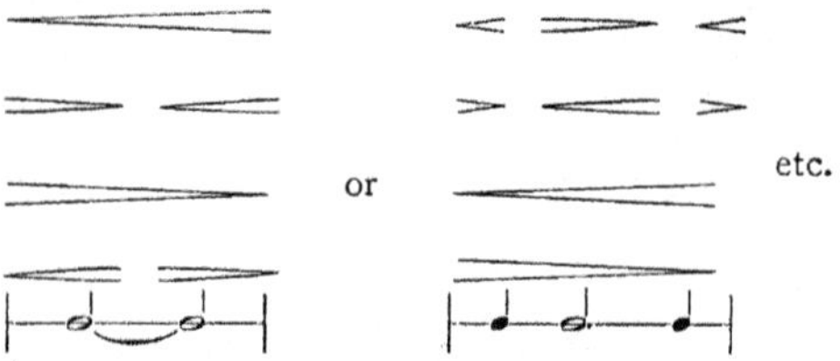

Right thigh.

Left thigh

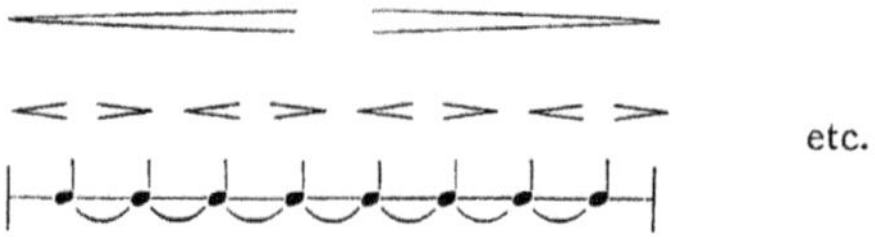

Buttocks.

Breathing.

CONTROL.

sf = ∧ = sforzando.

1. *Pathetic Accents.*—The pupil walks in a given time. At *Hopp* he accents one of the weak beats, either with the feet, with the arms, with the head, or by breathing, or on a strong beat increases the accent.

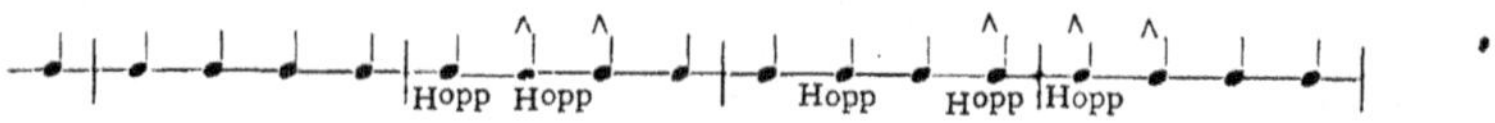

2. The pupils walk in a given time.

(*a*) At *Hopp* they make a or or *backward.*

(*b*) " " half turn.

" " whole turn.

(*c*) " they insert some prearranged rhythmic phrase.

E.g.: (the given rhythm being)

(*d*) The pupils walk in $\frac{8}{4}$. At *Hopp*, the bar they are walking must be completed with an mprovised rhythm.

E.g.: 

(*e*) The pupils step a given theme. At *Hopp* they step it backward, until the following *Iopp*, when they again walk forward.

(*f*) Given the theme at the first repetition the upils omit the last quaver, at the second repetition they omit two quavers, and so on until nly the figure remains. At *Hopp* they gradually reconstruct the theme in the same ray by adding the necessary quavers.

E.g.: 

AURAL EXERCISES.

The teacher plays, the pupils realise:

1. Rhythms with few notes and long rests.
2. Rhythms with *accelerando* and *ritardando.*
3. Rhythms with pathetic accents.

4. Rhythms composed of unequal bars.

5. Rhythms with *crescendo* and *diminuendo.*

The following are different ways of varying rhythms:

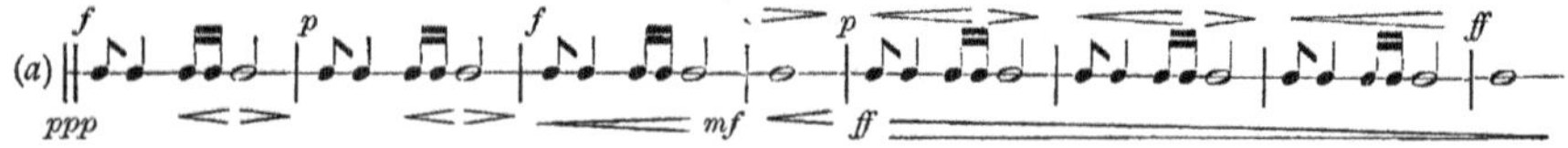

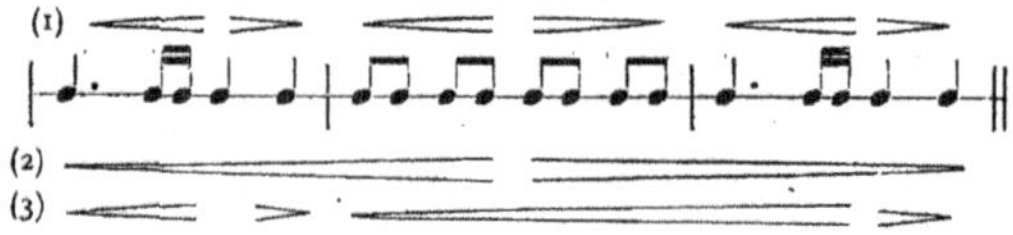

DIVISION OF LONG NOTE-VALUES INTO SHORTER VALUES OR INTO RHYTHMS.

6.

Teacher
Pupil

1st time: *lento.*
2nd time: *presto.*
3rd time: *allegretto,* etc.

7. Teacher
Pupil

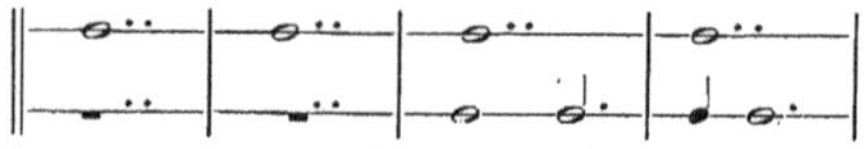

etc.

8. Consecutive realisation of bars in two alternated times.

Teacher
Pupil

9. The teacher plays a quick rhythm which is the counterpoint of a theme. The pupil inds the theme.

a) Teacher

Pupil

Counterpoint in semiquavers.

b) Teacher

Pupil

Counterpoint in semiquavers.

10. The teacher plays a two-bar phrase and repeats it three times. At the first repetition he pupil claps crotchet counterpoint; at the second repetition he steps quaver counterpoint; t the third repetition he combines the two.

'eacher

'upil

11. The teacher plays a slow theme. The pupil realises the counterpoint in notes half he length of the notes of the theme.

Teacher

Pupil

etc.

12. The teacher plays a theme in $\frac{12}{8}$, which the pupils realise, then the teacher accentuates the theme in such a way that it changes to $\frac{3}{2}$ and the pupils realise it in this time.

(*a*)
(*b*)

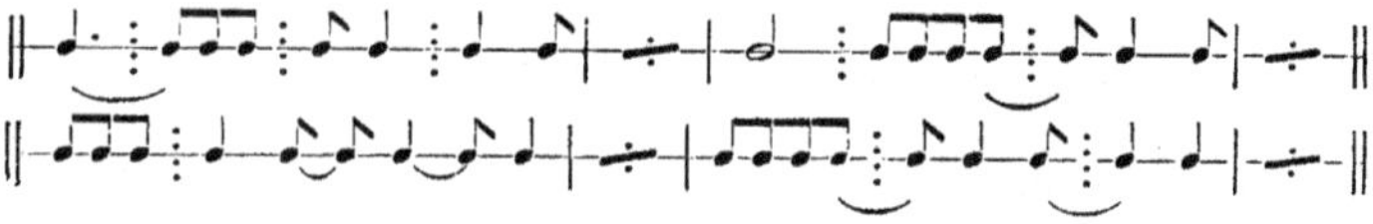

13. The teacher plays a theme several times. The pupils realise it. At *Hopp* they stand still, continuing the realisation in thought; at the next *Hopp* they resume the realisation in movement.

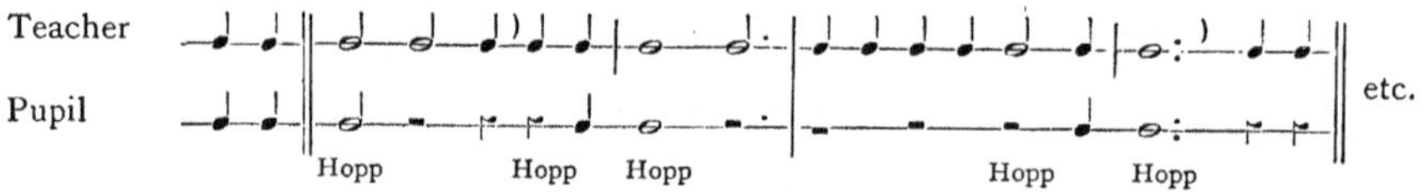

14. The teacher plays a chain of rhythms. The pupils realise the counterpoint in canon (♩, ♪, 𝅘𝅥𝅯, etc.).

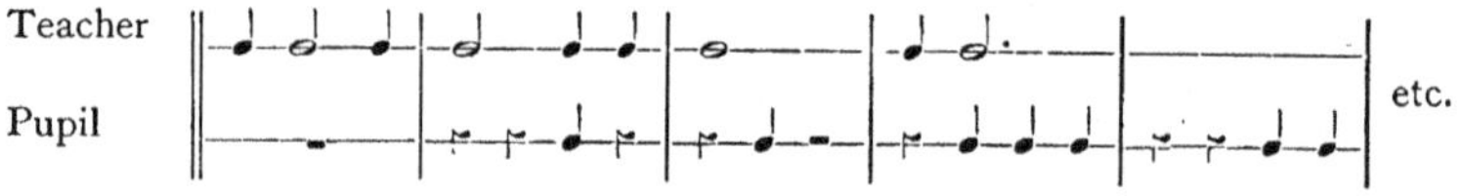

15. The teacher plays a slow theme. The pupils realise each bar, twice as fast and twice as slow, in canon.

IMPROVISATION.

A pupil improvises a theme in 8 time, *e.g.*: 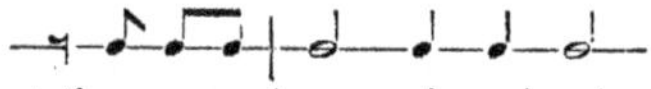

Another pupil repeats the same theme without the anacrusis: 

The class repeats the two bars one after the other. The result is two unequal bars, one in 8, the other in 6.

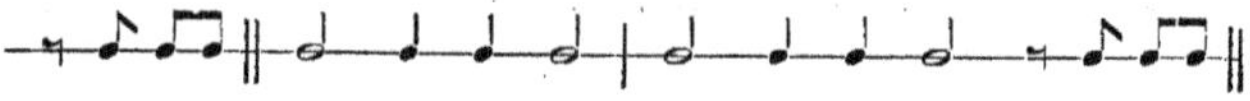

A third pupil realises the whole of the preceding theme with phrasing *crescendo* and *diminuendo*, and the class repeats it with the same nuances.

E.g.:

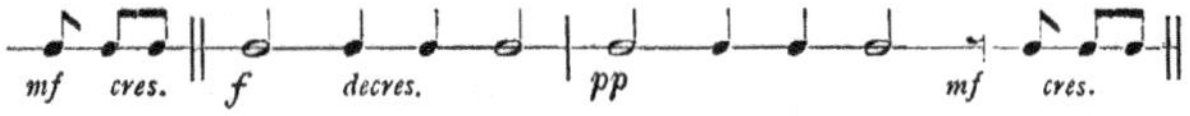

A fourth pupil adds pathetic accents.

E.g.:

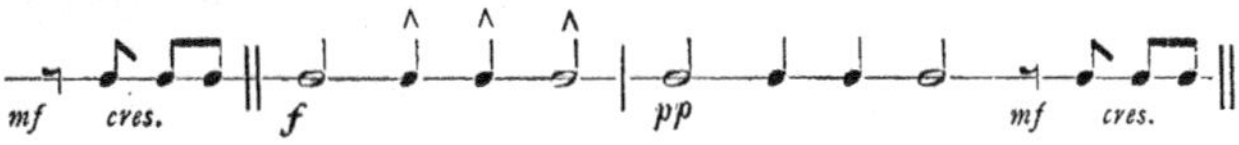

etc.

EXERCISES IN CONDUCTING.

1. A pupil conducts, introducing pathetic accents, *i.e.*, an increase of tension in the gesture which leads up to the accent on the following beat. The pupils realise these pathetic accents in one of the following ways:

(*a*) By a stamp of the foot.
(*b*) By an accentuation with the arm.
(*c*) By a turn of the trunk to right or left.
(*d*) By a movement of the head.
(*e*) By an inspiration.
(*f*) By rising on the toes (or by an accented bend of the knees).
(*g*) Or by bending the trunk backwards, etc.

2. A given theme is conducted by one pupil, the rest being separated into three groups. He divides the theme at will, directing one group to walk the first phrase, another to walk the second, and so on (only one group moves at a time).

E.g.:

etc.

3. The pupils are divided into two groups; the conductor stands between the groups, and indicates:

(*a*) For the left group a bar in $\frac{4}{4}$ with pathetic accents on a certain beat; for the right group a bar in $\frac{4}{4}$ with pathetic accents on a different beat, or:

(*b*) Left a bar in 8, right a bar in 6; left a bar in 4, right a bar in 5; left a bar in 3, right a bar in 7, etc.

FREE EXERCISES FOR THREE PUPILS.

1. A B C

2. A B C

N.B.—For all these exercises the pupils stand in three parallel lines. The pupils in each line hold hands.

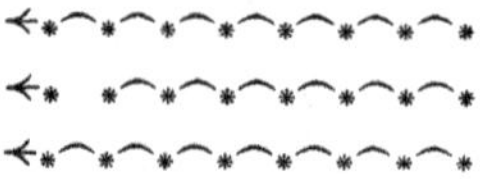

3. A B C

A B C

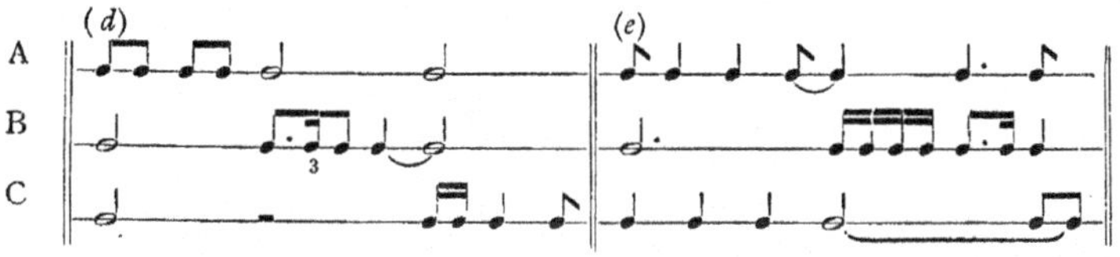

The lines A and C diverge and then approach each other again at the repeat.

Canon.

These canons can also be realised in *circles.*

FREE EXERCISE.

A = Starting-point common to groups 1, 2, & 3.

B = The moment at which 1 & 3 turn. (See sketch below.)

C = Meeting point of 1, 2, & 3.

D = Turning point of 1 & 3.

E = Final meeting point.

On 𝅗𝅥. stop, on ♩ half-turn. Then begin again in the opposite direction, interchanging rhythms. (The manner of skipping to be decided beforehand.)

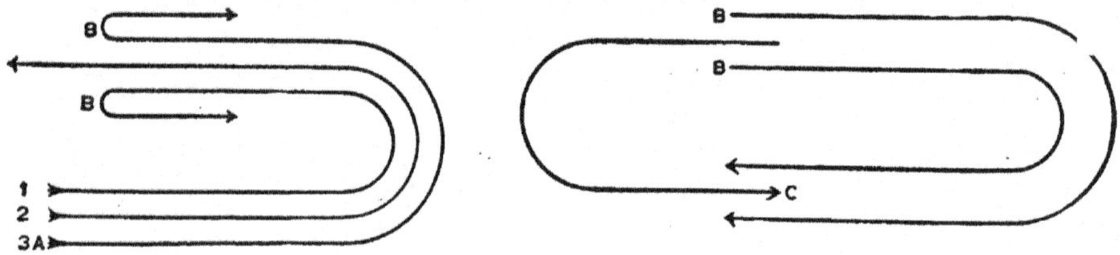

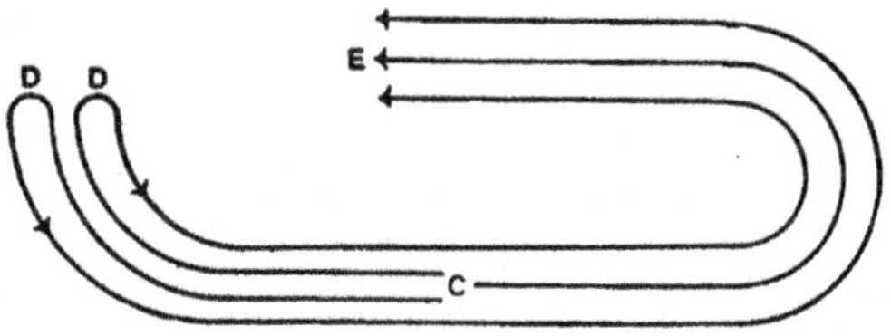

TABLE OF SYNCOPATED NOTE-VALUES.

The pupils are arranged in three double columns, moving in circles. 𝅝, 𝅗𝅥, ♩, and ♪, either simple or syncopated are to be realised by steps and bends, excepting notes marked + which are not to be subdivided.

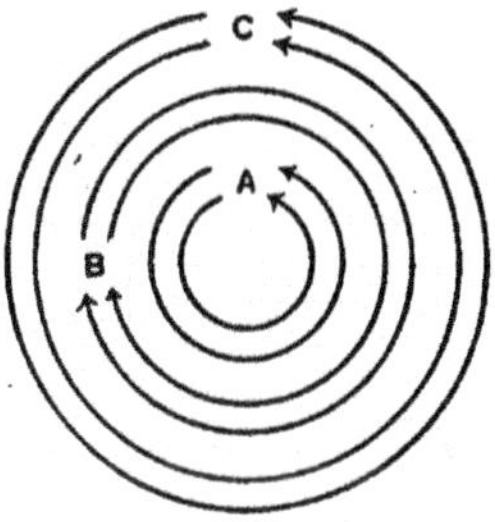

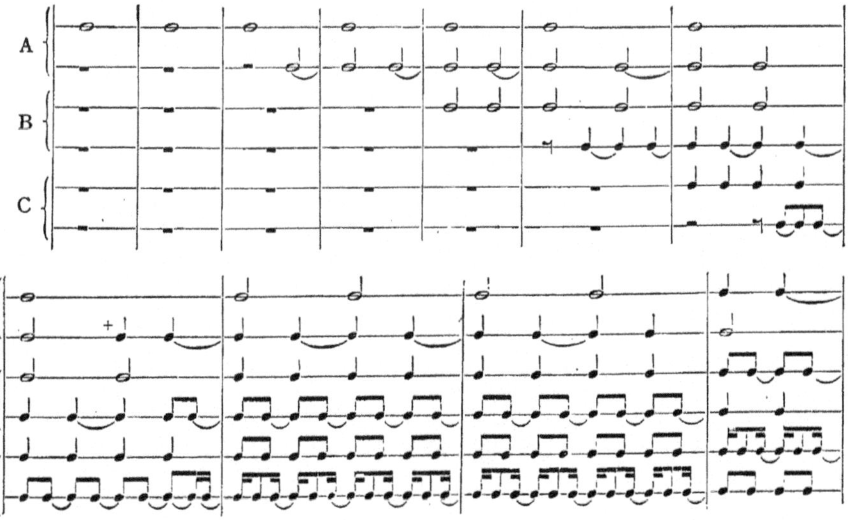

After the last step the pupils kneel.

See *Marches rythmiques*, Nos. 42-49. } Lausanne : Jobin et Cie.
Esquisses rythmiques. } London : Novello & Co.
La Plastique animée.

CHAPTER VIII.

NONUPLE TIME.

EXERCISES IN MARCHING WHILE BEATING TIME.

PREPARATORY EXERCISES.

From beat 1 to beat 6. As in the bar in $\frac{8}{4}$.
" " 6 " 7. The hands are raised at right-angles to the arm.
" " 7 " 9. As in 6 to 8 in $\frac{8}{4}$.

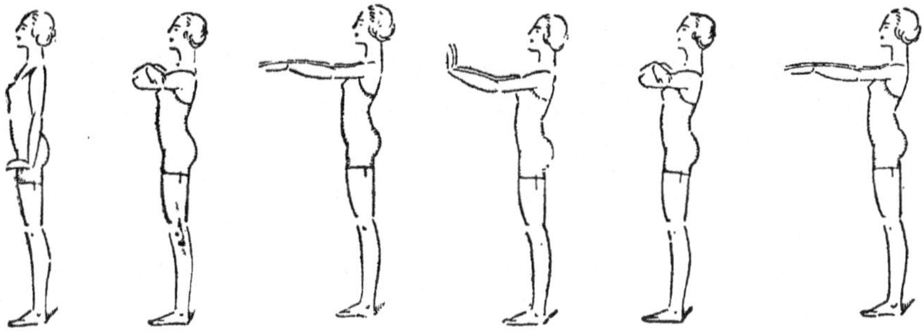

4. 5. 6.

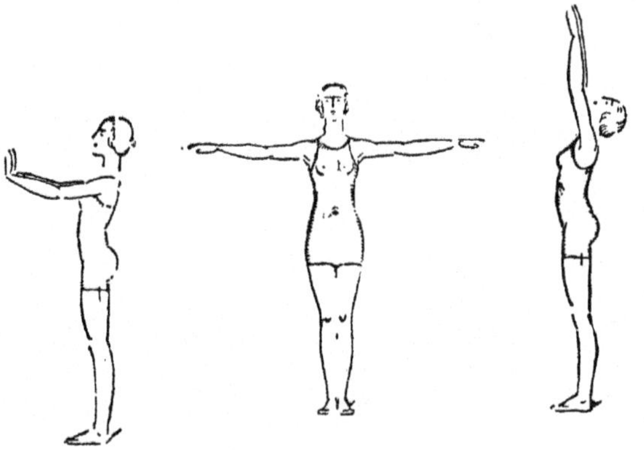

$\frac{9}{4}$

1. (*a*) 

(*b*) with quavers.

(*c*) with semiquavers.

(*d*) with demisemiquavers.

$\frac{27}{8}$

2. 

3. 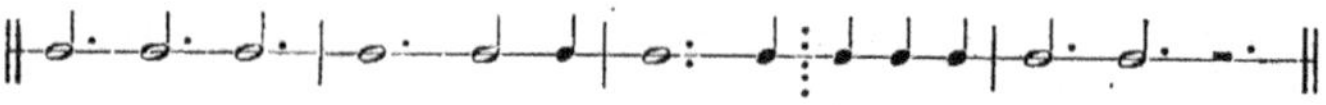

4. 

PERIODS AND RESTS.

1. 

2. 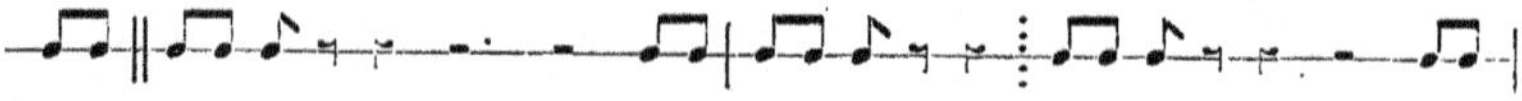

3. 

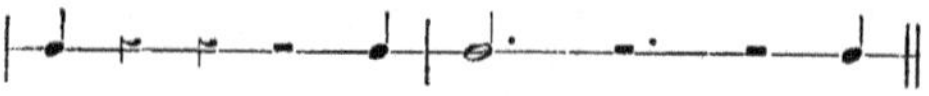

4. 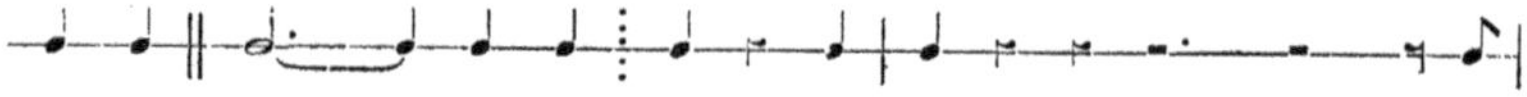

5. Three bars in $\frac{3}{4}$, without beating time.

Exercise : *The Candles.*

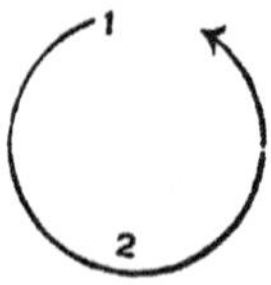

On 1st beat of the 4th bar all stop marching and shut their eyes.
" " " the 1st pupil kneels.
" " 5th bar the 2nd pupil kneels.
" " 6th bar the 3rd pupil kneels.
" " 7th bar the 1st pupil rises and opens his eyes.
" " following bar, the 2nd pupil rises and opens his eyes, and so on until all the pupils have risen. As they get up the pupils raise their arms (on 1).

UNITY OF STYLE

From a given theme A composed of notes of different lengths, make up 8 bars, using only the elements contained in the theme, but placed differently, repeated, alternated, etc.

E.g.:

elements :

3 elements :

3 elements :

3 elements :

3 elements :

3 elements : 11.

TWELVE-BAR PHRASES.

3 × 4 = 12

1.

4 × 3 = 12

2.

5 + 5 + 2 = 12

3a

5 + 2 + 5 = 12

3*b*. Like 3*a*, but the two-bar phrase between the two five-bar phrases.

3*c*. Like 3*a*, but the two-bar phrase at the beginning.

ANALYSIS OF NOTE-VALUES.

The note of 9 beats |◌| :

Execution: 1, 2, 3, 4, 5. As in the notes of 7 and 8 beats.

6. The free leg is stretched still further back; the supporting leg bends more.

7, 8, 9, As 6, 7, 8, in the note of 8 beats.

The note $\frac{27}{8}$

Same execution as in the note of nine beats.

THE EXECUTION OF GIVEN THEMES

THREE TIMES AS FAST AND AS SLOW.

(Without subdivision of the longer note-values.)

See triple time ($\frac{3}{4}$), Vol. 1, page 31 *et seq.*

1. *With the same length of bar.*—The arms do *not* participate in the change of time. The feet step the rhythm :

Once in the original time;
Three times in three times as fast; } Same length of bar.
Nine times in nine times as fast.

(a) 

and vice versâ

(b) 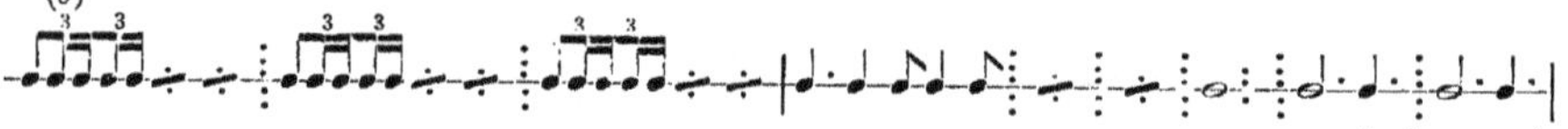

and vice versâ.

2. *With change of bar.*—Repeat exercises 1*a* and 1*b*, the arms now beating each change of bar-time.

3. *With anacrusic themes.*—The new time begins with the anacrusis. The arms beat as in (2).

(a) 

b) 

4. *The same with syncopation* (difficult), etc., etc.

PERIODS WITH BARS OF REST OF UNEQUAL DURATION.

1.–4. 

Let the pupils know beforehand the number of bars.

BREATHING.

See Vol. 1, page 19.

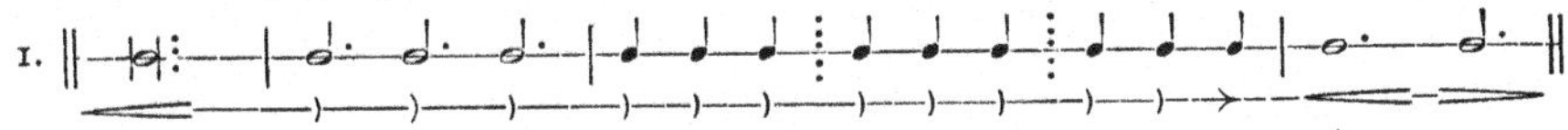

2. Play a musical phrase several times to the pupils, then ask them to phrase it with breathing.

3. After a deep inspiration sing some note of the scale several times with a feeling of supporting the voice (during the expiration):

(1.) On the feet, firmly pressed on the ground.
(2). On the calves.
(3.) On the thighs.
(4.) On the arms (fists closed).
(5.) On the whole body.

N.B.—During expiration strongly contract that part of the body on which thought has been concentrated.

INDEPENDENCE OF THE LIMBS.

The note-values  are to be studied separately then the pupils will realise them in sequence, subdividing them.

The arms will beat time in canon:

1. One beat after the feet.
2. One beat before the feet.

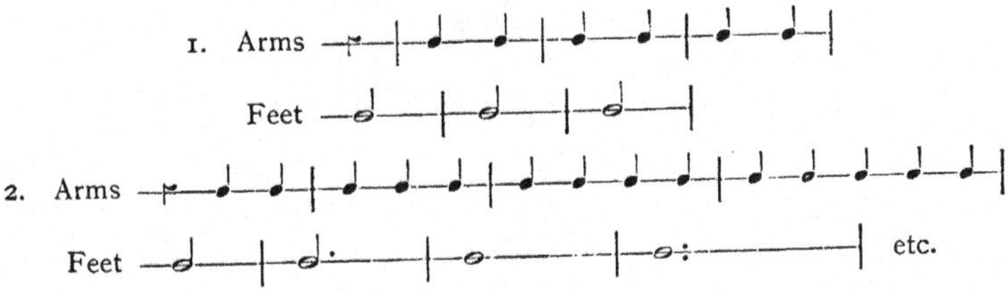

3, 4. As in 1 and 2, the arms beginning one beat earlier than the feet.

5. Repeat all the exercises of the preceding chapters, replacing the movements  and  by the following movements:

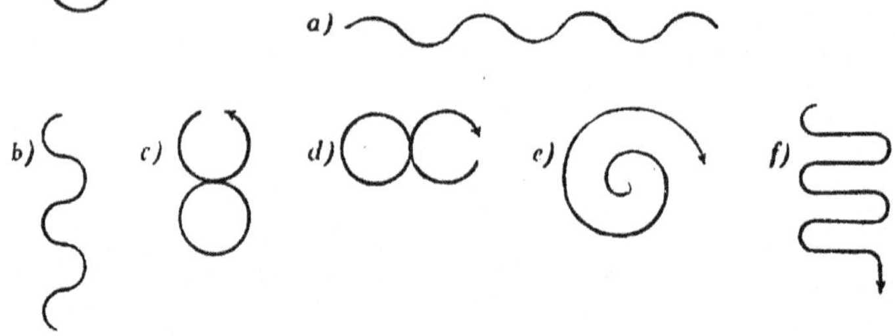

CONTROL AND INHIBITION.

1. The pupils realise the note 𝅗𝅥. beating $\frac{3}{4}$. At *Hopp* either { the arms or the feet } stop for one beat, so that a canon results; at the next *Hopp* the same, till the arms and feet come together again.

2. Repeat exercise 1 with the notes 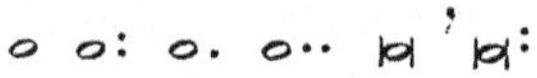

3. The pupil walks slowly in ♩

At the command	*two,*	he makes		once.
,,	*three,*	,,		
,,	*four,*	,,		
,,	*five,*	,,		
,,	*six,*	,,		
,,	*seven,*	,,		
,,	*eight,*	,,		
,,	*nine,*	,,		

4. The pupils walk and beat in $\frac{5}{4}$. At *Hopp* they omit one of the arm-movements continuing to accent in $\frac{5}{4}$ so that all the gestures 2, 3, 4, and 5 will be accented in turn on beat 1.

5. The same exercise, the feet realising 𝅝:

EXERCISES IN HEARING AND REALISING.

The teacher plays themes.

1. The pupils step the counterpoint: (*a*) in triplets, (*b*) in semiquavers, (*c*) in skipping steps.

E.g.;

2. The pupils realise a given theme with their arms, using the gestures for beating time, whilst the feet walk quavers.

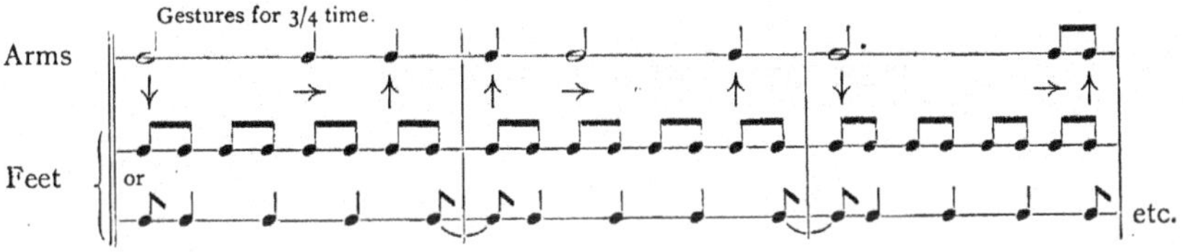

DIVISION INTO SHORTER NOTE-VALUES.

1st, *allegretto;* 2nd, *adagio;* 3rd, *allegro molto,* etc.

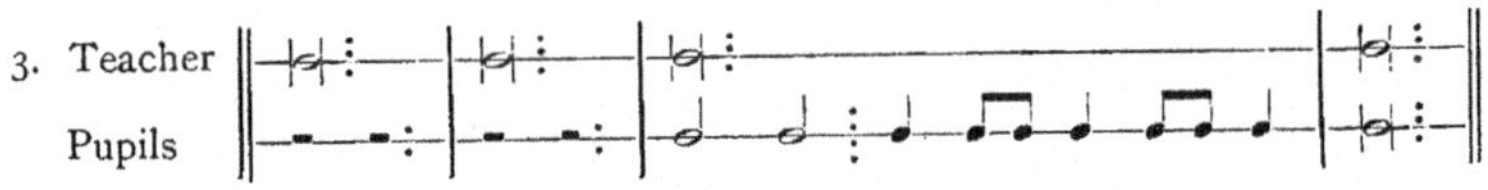

SYNCOPATION.

The following phrase to be studied and realised.

QUICK THEMES TO BE REALISED THREE AND FOUR TIMES AS SLOW.

The theme is played three or four times; at *Hopp* the pupils realise it three or four times as slow.

Four times as slow.

Four times as slow.

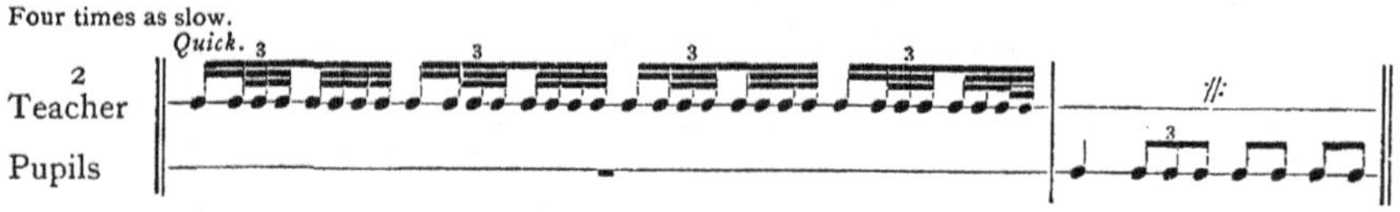

Three times as slow.

Four times as slow.

Three times as slow.

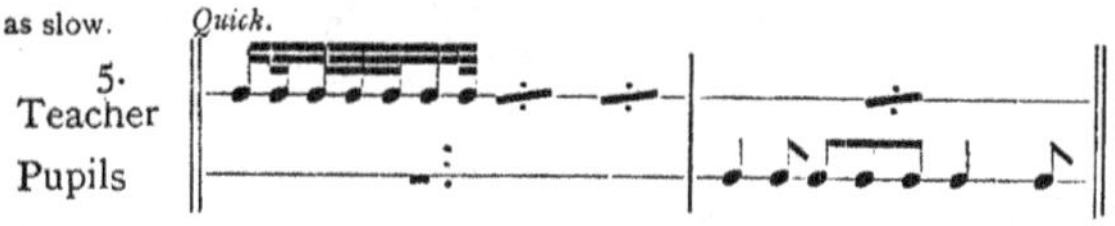

Three times as slow.

APPOGGIATURAS.

The lower appoggiaturas consist of a semitone :

1. The pupils walk in threes (A, B, C) holding hands. At *Hopp* (or according to a given rhythm) A (B or C) sings an upper or lower appoggiatura and interprets it plastically by a step forward; on the resolution A (B or C) stands still and the others make a step.

E.g. :

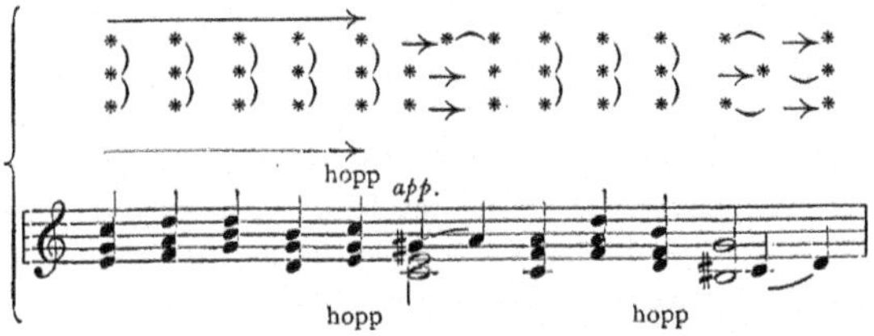

Sequence of chords to be used with appoggiaturas.

2. The pupils, with arms crossed, walk in a circle. The teacher plays a sequence of chords. At *Hopp* he plays an appoggiatura ; the pupils interpret it by standing still and substituting arm-gestures for the step. On the resolution the pupils start walking again. The arms are kept in the same position until the following *Hopp*, when a new gesture is made (use gestures for the bar in 5 or 6 time).

3. Pupils stand still and interpret the appoggiatura by a movement of the head, or by breathing, then make a step to interpret the resolution of the appoggiatura.

RETARDATIONS.

Pupils walk in threes, holding hands, singing a series of chords. At *Hopp* (or according to some prearranged rhythm) one of the voices sings a retardation, the pupil interpreting it plastically by standing still, the two others making a step forward. On the resolution these two stand still and the one who was singing the retardation makes a step.

INTERVALS AND CHORDS.

The pupils stand in four columns:

*	*	*	*
*	*	*	*
*	*	*	*
*	*	*	*
*	*	*	*
contraltos	altos	mezzo-sopranos	sopranos

basses, baritones, 2nd tenors, 1st tenors.
basses, tenors, altos, sopranos.

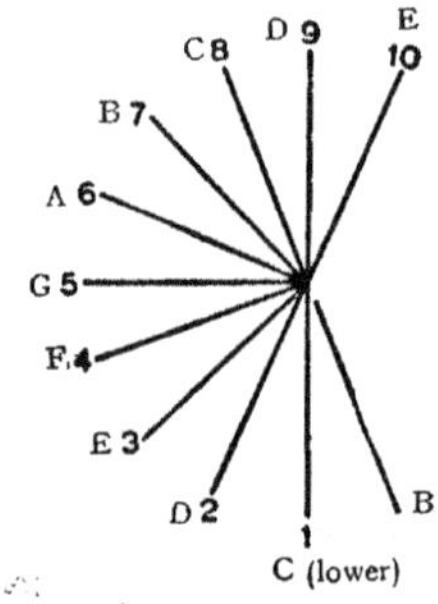

They all advance singing in *unison*, and showing the pitch of the sounds by the nine movements of the arms shown on page 4 (a gesture No. 10 can be added, arms raised and stretched behind the head. The low B can be interpreted by a gesture of the arms made by stretching them out behind the body).

Each interval is interpreted by varying lengths of steps.

A minor 2nd by step No. 1.
A major 2nd by step No. 2.
A 3rd by step No. 3.
A 4th by step No. 4.
A 5th by step No. 5.
A 6th by step No. 6 (exceptional number).

When a large interval is to be sung, the weight of the body is brought forward. When the melody rises, the steps are made forward, when it falls, backward. Thus when the pupils sing chords, a great variety of grouping and lines will be formed, owing to the different arm-movements and steps.

E.g.:

UNEQUAL BARS CONTAINING THE SAME UNIT OF QUAVER OR SEMIQUAVER.

Realise and write down the exercises at the end of this volume.

TWO-PART EXERCISES.

The teacher plays a theme in two parts (one voice with the R.H. and the other with the L.H.).

The pupils clap the higher voice and march the lower.

1. 

2. 

3. 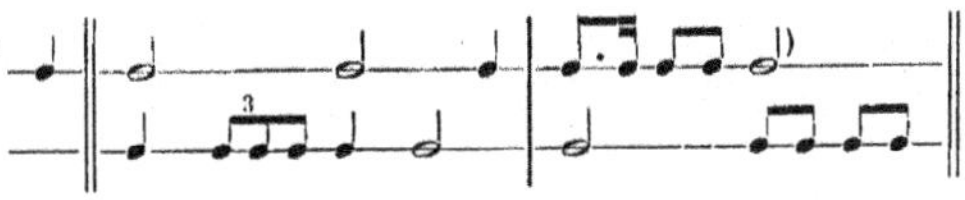 etc., etc.

The pupils write down the rhythms studied during the lesson.

IMPROVISATION.

A pupil improvises:

1. A theme with phrasing and dynamic changes.
2. A theme, part of which is taken three times as fast or as slow.

E.g.: 

Lento.

or 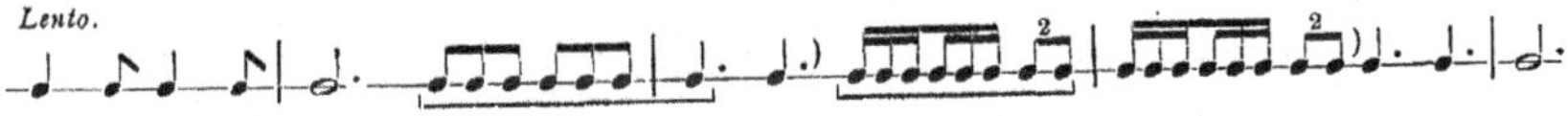

3. A theme with syncopations.
4. A theme in which each bar consists of shorter note-values than the last.
5. A theme containing rests which are realised by breathing.
6. A theme with kneeling, walking backward, springs, pirouettes, etc.

The class repeats the motives which have been improvised.

EXERCISES IN CONDUCTING.

1. A pupil conducts:

   Rhythms doubling or tripling } the quickness or slowness.

   (*a*) Beginning on the first beat.

   (*b*) Beginning with an anacrusis.

2. A rapid theme with pathetic accents shown by movements of the wrist.

E.g.:

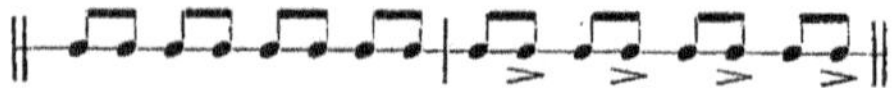

or

etc., etc.

CONDUCTING MELODIES SUNG BY THE PUPILS.

(With the whole body.)

The pupils learn a melody by heart. One of them conducts it, using his own interpretation as to nuances and phrasing, while the others follow his lead, singing. The conductor must use such gestures or attitudes as will enable him to give an intelligent rendering of the melody.

MELODIES FOR CONDUCTING WITH THE BODY.

1.

2.

3.

4.

5.

For 2 persons.

6.

Further melodies for conducting in this manner will be found at the end of this volume, and also in *Exercices de plastique animée.*

A NEW SERIES OF GESTURES.

A study of these twenty consecutive gestures will give the pupil an enlarged vocabulary of movement for plastic interpretation.

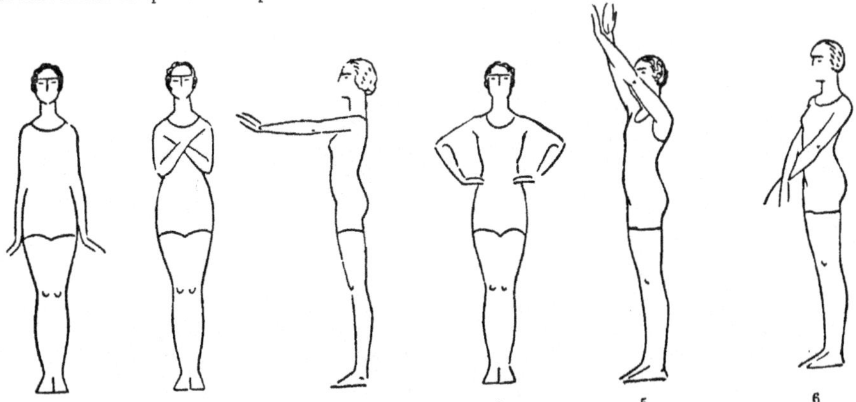

1 2 3 4 5 6

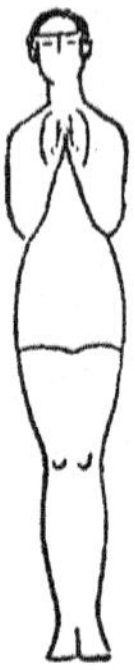
7

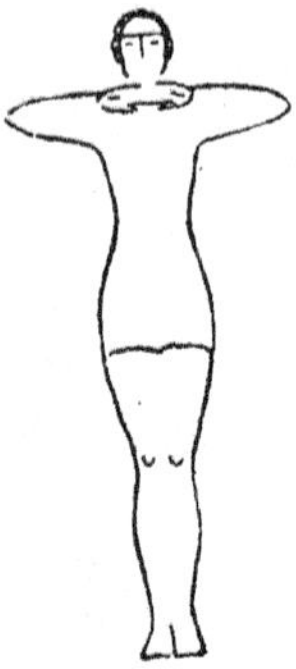
8

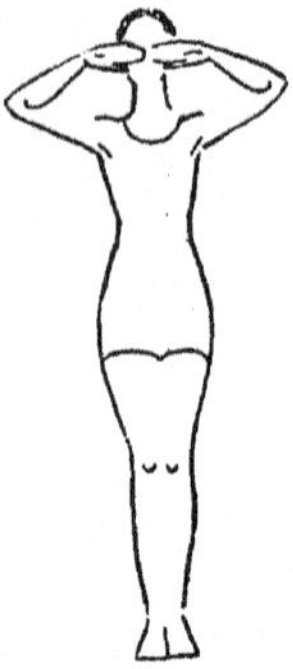
9

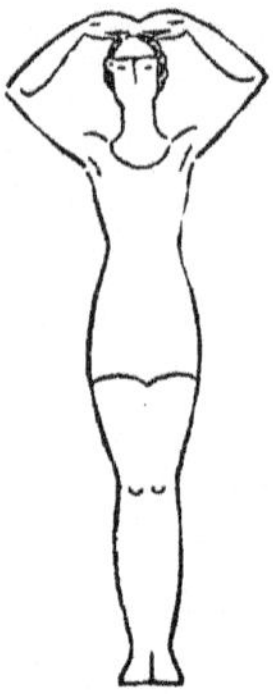
10

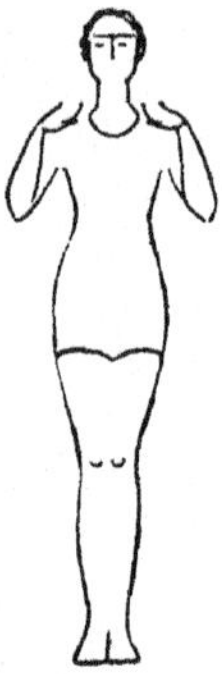
11

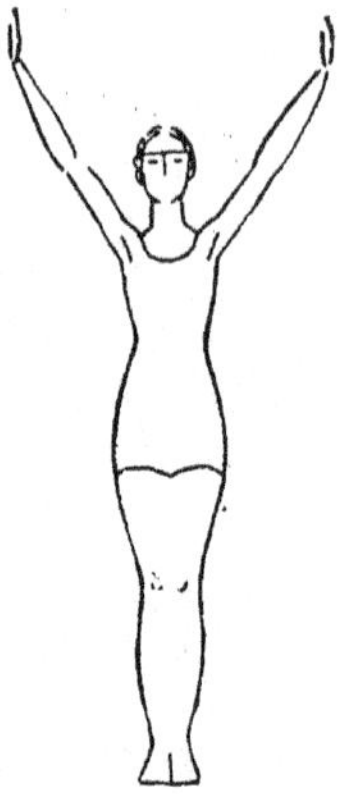
12

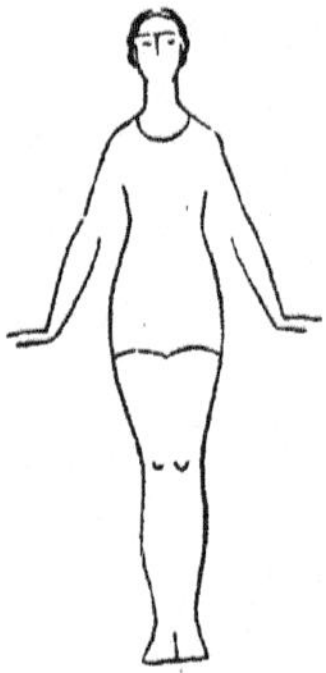
13

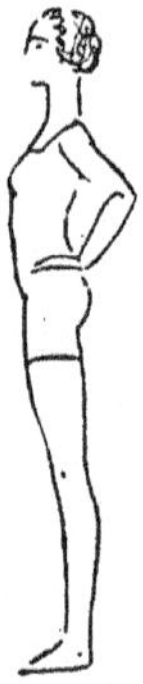
14

15

16

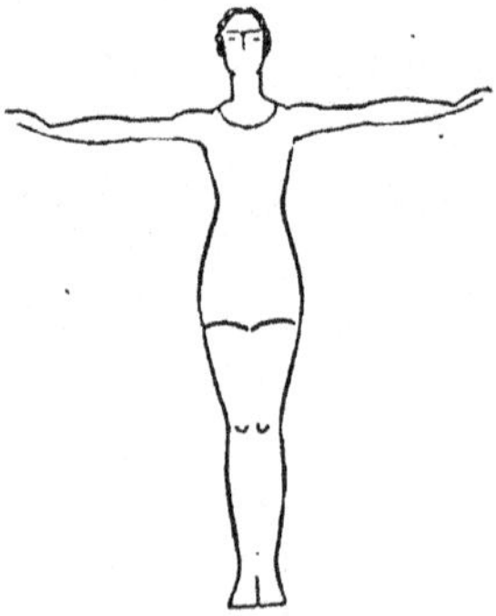
17

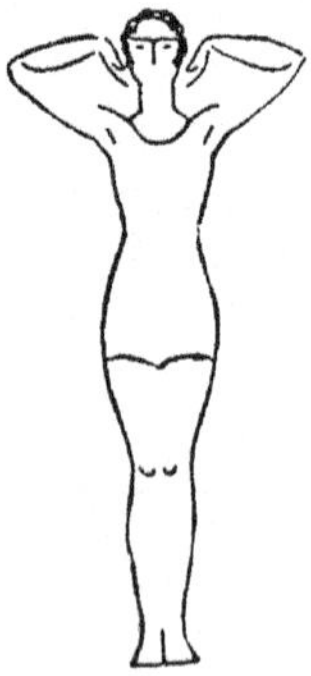
18

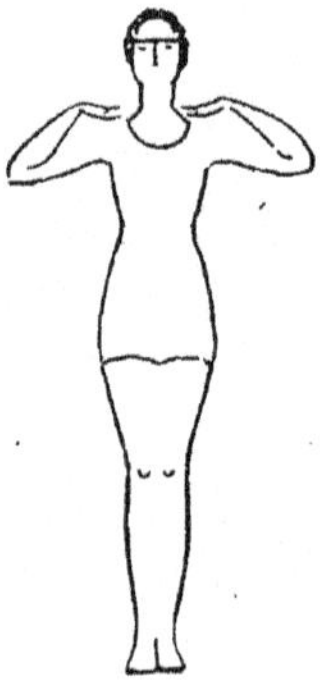
19

20

These twenty gestures should be studied.

(1) In their logical sequence.

(2) In canon (there are twenty posssible combinations, thus giving great variety).

(3) Associating them with the various movements of the legs used to show the notes of from 4 to 9 beats.

FREE EXERCISES.

ESTIMATION OF SPACE.

A definite space having been decided on, within the limits of which a rhythm is to be realised, the pupil must estimate the space and neither exceed nor understep the limits.

1. (*a*) Cross the room in ten steps (the length of which must be estimated beforehand).
   (*b*) The same with twelve, eight, six, etc.
   (*c*) The same, stopping exactly in the middle of the given space.
   (*d*) The same, stopping exactly two-thirds across the given space.
   (*e*) The same, realising a rhythm 

2. While realising a rhythm, describe with the feet a geometrical figure in a fixed given space, a circle, triangle, square, rectangle, etc.

3. Repeat the above exercises with the eyes shut.

4. Several groups describe very simple figures, trying not to get in each others way, etc.

5. Two pupils move round the room following lines settled in advance and punctuating them by attitudes. The other pupils repeat from memory.

6. A group runs quavers then stops, standing, kneeling, raising the arms, in a lunging pose, etc. A second group follows, trying to assume a position complementary to that of the first group. The third and fourth groups move in their turn and complete the figure sketched by the two first.

A DANCE.

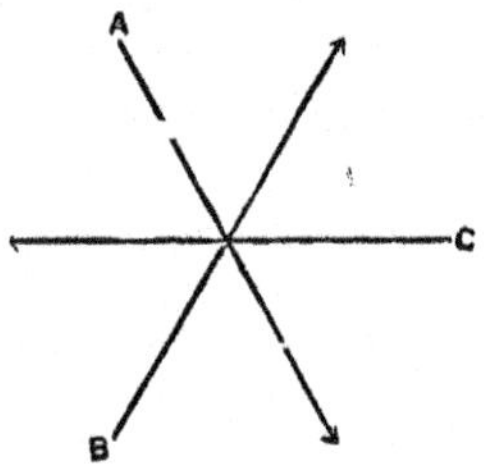

The pupils are divided into three groups A, B, C. They skip and run in canon twice:

On the 3rd beat of the 1st thetic bar, the 2nd group enters (group B); on the 3rd beat of the 2nd thetic bar, the 3rd group enters (group C).

The centre is reached at the note 𝅝. Then the line is continued in the same direction to the outer edge.

Use skipping-step No. 2.

During the  raise the arms and gradually bend the back and head backwards. At the stopping point  lower the arms slowly to the horizontal position sideways.

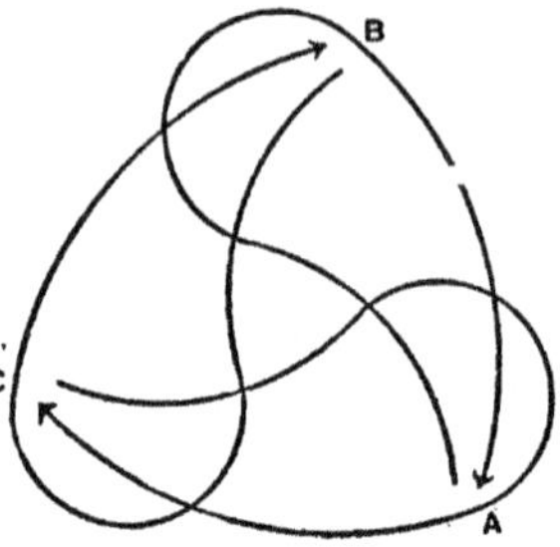

♩. = ♩ *Variation of the preceding rhythm.*

This variation follows immediately on the first theme. It is realised twice as a canon, according to the lines in the second figure.

Skipping-step No. 4.

Then the leaders of the three groups, A, B, C, come to the centre by a spiral line.

(A)

(B)

(C)

Skipping step No. 1.

When A, B, C meet in the centre they begin the following rhythm:

A, B, C moving in a circle

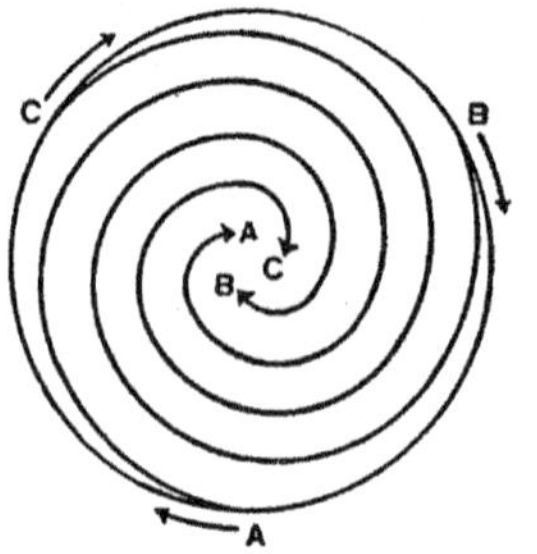

The skipping-step changes; once No. 1, upper part of the body bent forward; once No. 4, upper part of the body bent backward.

The  should be realised once with the upper part of the body bent backward, and once with the upper part of the body bent forward.

Here is the complete canon:

A

B

C

The same canon in a shorter space:

ANOTHER GAME.

The children are divided into four circles, A, B, C, D, one within another:

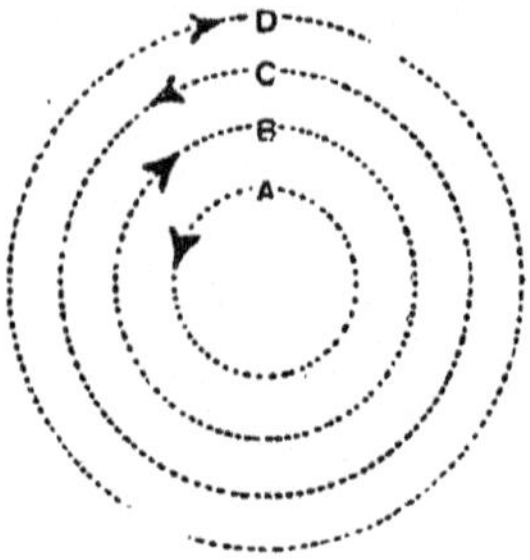

Circle A realises the following rhythm:

Circle B realises the same rhythm beginning at the second bar.

Circle C „ „ „ „ „ third „

Circle D „ „ „ „ „ fourth „

(At the beginning the four circles are kneeling down.)

The same game can be realised in six bars:

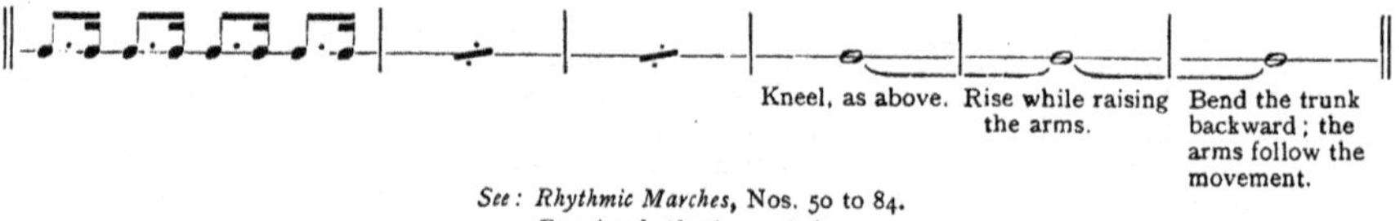

See: Rhythmic Marches, Nos. 50 to 84.
Exercises de plastique animée.
Esquisses Rhythmiques pour piano.

CHAPTER IX.

SUGGESTIONS FOR THE COMPOSITION OF NEW EXERCISES.

REALISATION IN CANON.

1. $\frac{3}{4}$, $\frac{6}{8}$ alternating.

e.g.:

Ditto $\frac{3}{2}$, $\frac{12}{8}$.

e.g.:

Ditto, with unequal bars.

Example:

2. Introducing rests.

Example:

3. *Phrases.*—The teacher plays a certain number of bars forming a phrase. The pupil, who begins to realise at *hopp*, has to memorise not one bar only but a whole phrase.

Ditto, with phrases composed of two themes, A and B, each phrase finishing with a bar of rests, of longer note-values, or of a contrasting rhythm.

4. *Twice as fast and twice as slow.*—Supposing that quadruple time is chosen, the teacher plays a rhythm on the 3rd and 4th beats, which the pupil has to realise twice as slowly on beats 1, 2, 3, and 4 of the next bar.

Or vice versâ.—The teacher plays a rhythm in quadruple time and the pupil realises it twice as fast on the 1st and 2nd beats of the following bar.

Dittò, three times as fast or slow.

E.g. :
Teacher
Pupil

or

Teacher
Pupil

5. Unequal beats.

6. Double canon, in which the feet realise one bar later, the arms two bars later.

Teacher
Pupil

7. Canon, in which the pupil realises counterpoint as well as theme (one by clapping, the other by walking).

E.g. :

8. Realisation two beats later.

E.g.:

Ditto, one beat later.

9. Canon with singing.

10. Canon with expression.—The teacher plays a theme with expression, which the pupi realises one bar later, paying special attention to the nuances and dynamics.

E.g.:

11. Canon with polyrhythm.

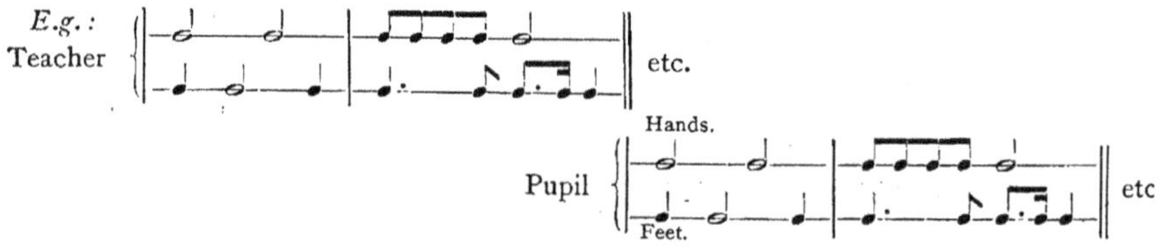

12. *Realisation two bars later.*

E.g.:

eacher

upil

etc.

13. *Canon of gestures with plastic realisation.*—One pupil improvises a series of gestures hich the class imitates one bar later. The teacher improvises at the pianoforte following the ıances indicated by the gestures of the soloist.

14. *Canon,* in which the pupils realise the rhythms played in the treble by walking rward, those played in the bass by walking backward.

15. *Canon* composed of unequal bars in 2, 3, 4, 5, 6 time, etc.

COUNTERPOINT.

1. The pupil sings the scale of C or any other scale in a given rhythm and walks crotchet ıunterpoint to this theme. At *Hopp* he walks the rhythm and sings the counterpoint.

E.g.:

2. A theme being given, the pupils walk in syncopation to each note of it in double time.

E.g.:

etc.

3. The teacher plays a chain of rhythms; the pupils realise the counterpoint (♩ or ♪) canon.

E.g.:

eacher

ıpil

etc.

4. Each note of the counterpoint is realised in a different way; the first by an arm movement, the second by the foot, or by the head, or by the whole body, etc.

5. The pupils invent a free counterpoint to a given theme, trying above all, by their step and gestures, to make it a contrast to the theme.

E.g.:

Theme

Counterpoint

etc.

6. The pupils walk ♩ counterpoint to a given theme and at Hopp change to ♪ counterpoin

E.g.:

et

7. Counterpoint in quintuplets, sextuplets, etc.

E.g.:

etc.

8. The first beat of a theme to be realised by counterpoint in quintuplets, the rest i septuplets, and so on alternately.

9. Pupils take hands in couples; one realises the theme, the other the counterpoint. T former guides the latter, making him go backward, round in a circle, etc.

E.g.:

The same exercise should be done, the pupil who steps the counterpoint having his ey closed.

10. A given series of gestures is realised with double counterpoint, one part being sung, the other stepped:

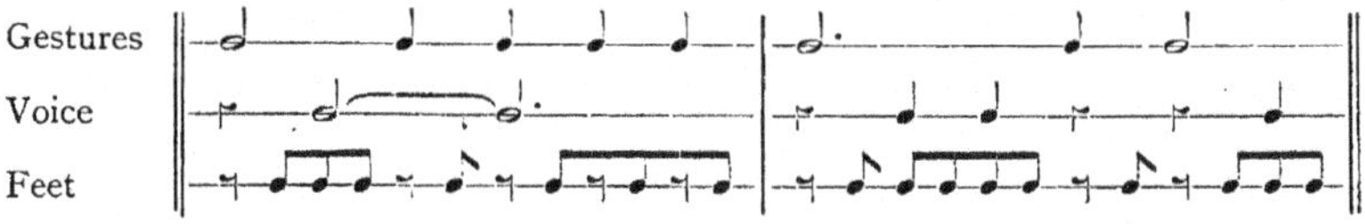

TWICE AND THREE TIMES AS FAST AND SLOW.

1. The pupil realises the theme with both arms and the feet; at *Hopp* the theme is taken two or three times as fast or slow with the feet or with one arm.

2. The teacher plays crotchets in any time. At *Hipp* the pupil steps one of the crotchets twice as fast; at *Hopp*, twice as slow.

The same three times as fast or slow.

3. The pupil does the twenty gestures with both arms. At *Hopp*, or in accordance with a prearranged rhythm, one arm makes the gestures two or three times as fast or slow.

4. The pupils realise a rhythm with arms and feet, breathing regularly in each bar. At *Hopp* they continue to realise with arms and feet but breathe twice as fast or slow.

5. A theme is given composed of several rhythmic elements; at *Hopp* one of these elements is done twice as fast or slow.

E.g.:

6. A rhythm is given composed of the following figure ♪. At *Hipp* the pupil steps one of the rhythmic figures twice as fast; at *Hopp* one twice as slow.

E.g.: 

etc.

7. The five crotchets in a bar of quintuple time are realised by the arms and feet simultaneously; at *Hopp* one arm (or the feet) realises them twice as fast.

E.g.:  etc., and vice versâ.

8. The arms realise a theme with dynamic nuances.

E.g.: 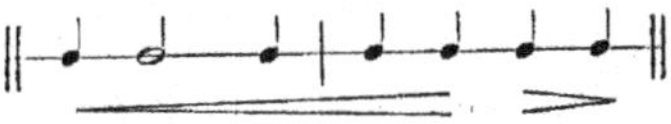

At *Hopp*, one arm realises the theme twice as fast, still keeping to the original nuances.

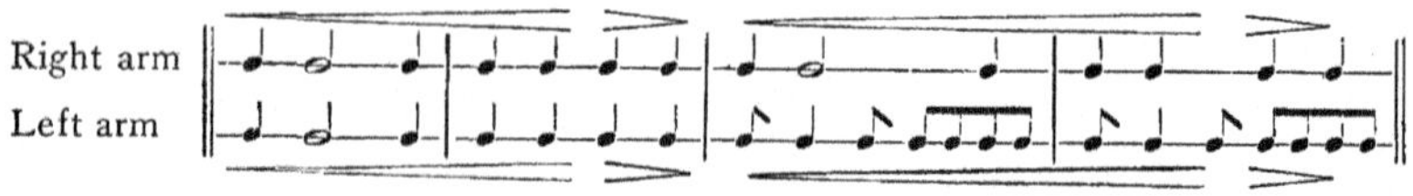

All the preceding exercises can be realised, the pupils walking in three files, one of the files realising two or three times as fast or slow at *Hopp*.

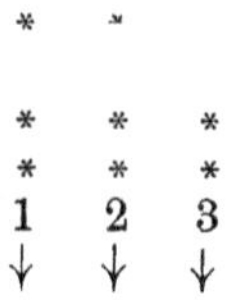

9. The teacher plays a theme consisting of unequal beats. At *Hopp* the pupils realise the following beat two or three times as fast or slow.

10. The teacher plays a semibreve three times. The pupils then realise a given theme three times over in the given duration of time.

11. The pupils realise a series of any five gestures with both arms; then five times as fast with one arm, while the other continues in the original tempo.

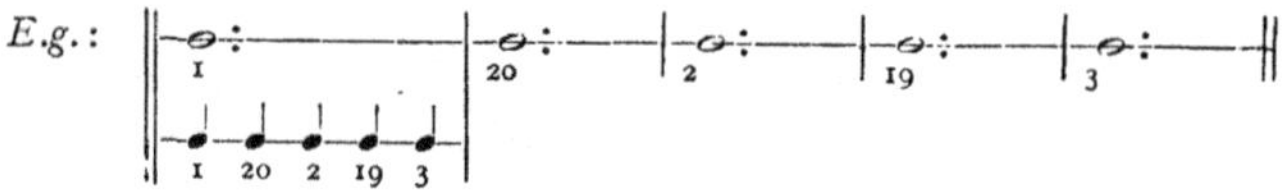

Other series: 18, 4, 17, 5, 16; 6, 15, 7, 13, 8; 12, 9, 11, 10, 18, etc.

12. The teacher plays five bars in quintuple time; the pupil realises them five times as fast in the time of one bar.

or vice versâ.

13. A series of rhythms in sextuple time is given; at *Hopp* the pupil steps the first three beats twice as fast or slow, or the last three beats three times as fast or slow.

E.g.:

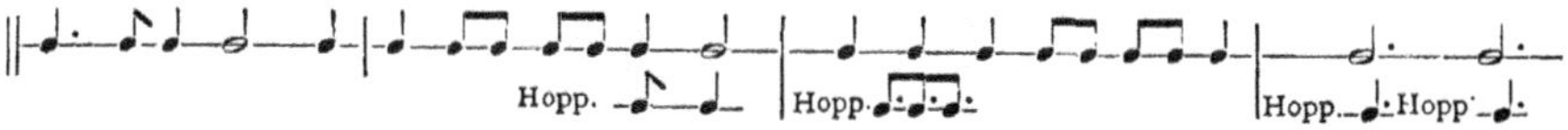

14. A theme in simple time is given, one beat of which consists of a triplet. At *Hopp* the pupil takes the ♪ of the triplet as the tempo for the ♪'s in the following bar.

E.g.:

etc.

or vice versâ:

etc.

15. An anacrusic theme being given, the pupil, at *Hopp*, realises either the anacrusis or the thesis two or three times as fast or slow.

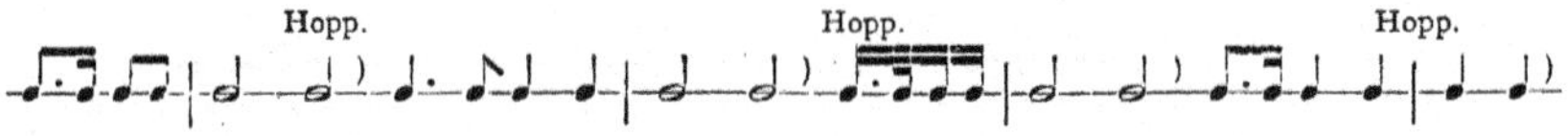

etc.

PHRASING.

1. The pupils stand in a line, each representing one note of the scale. One pupil calls out several "notes" and makes them sing a chord.

2. The pupils realise with one arm a period phrased in a prearranged way, and with the other a different period differently phrased.

The same exercise should be carried out by the feet and one arm, by the feet and the voice, or by the arms and the voice.

3. Three different phrasings to be carried out simultaneously.

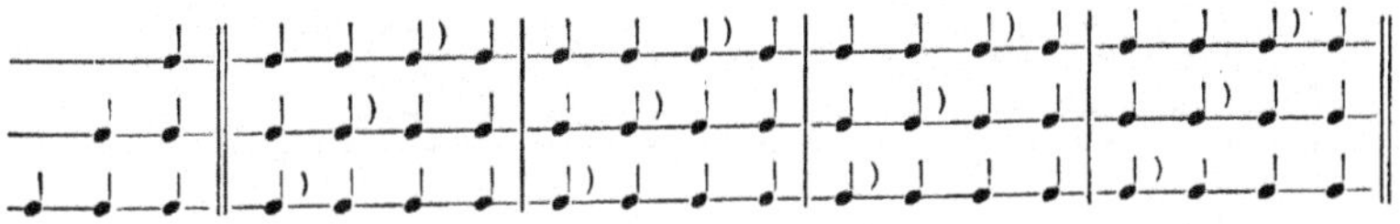

4. The pupils sing a phrase and at the same time realise it in canon with gestures.

E.g.:

5. The pupils learn four little rhythmic elements,

E.g.: 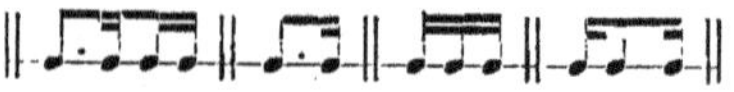

then, from these elements, the teacher constructs a series of phrases, which the pupils try to memorise and realise.

E.g.:

INHIBITION.

1. Beat 4 against 3, or step 4 whilst beating 3. At *Hopp* omit one beat.

The same 3 against 2, 5 against 3, etc.

2. Beat 3 with the left arm and 3 twice as fast with the right arm. At *Hopp* omit one beat.

3. Pupils take hands in couples and run quavers. The teacher calls out two numbers between 1 and 20 (the twenty gestures); the first pupil does the gesture indicated by the first number, the second pupil that indicated by the second number. They stand still facing one another and try to form a coherent group.

E.g.:

Pupil I.
Pupil II.

The same with three numbers and three pupils.

JUDGING DISTANCE.

1. The pupils, placed in three files, run quavers, and at *Hopp* form a prearranged geometrical figure, to be completed in a certain number of bars.

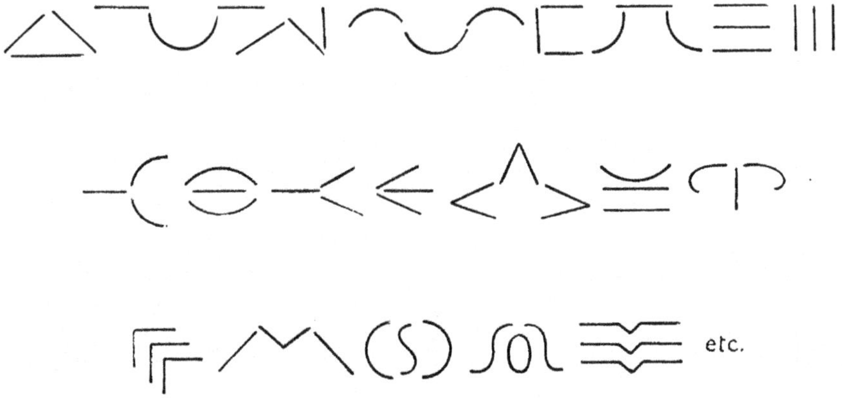

This should be combined with kneeling, raising or bending of the trunk, etc.

ACCENTUATION.

1. The teacher plays a series of quavers, some of which are accented. The pupils step only the accented notes.

E.g.:

The same with gestures.

The same, the teacher playing only the unaccented notes.

2. The teacher plays a series of quavers, some of which are accented. The pupils realise the accents by stamping with the same foot.

E.g.:

A phrase is interpreted by several groups, conducted by one pupil, who indicates by gestures that first one group then another is to advance, retire, step to the right or left, kneel, etc.

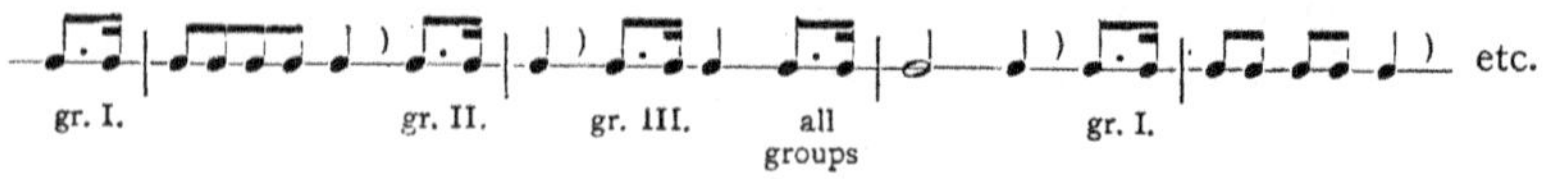

(See melodies for conducting at the end of the volume.)

EXERCISES IN PLASTIC.

See the two volumes published by MM. Jobin & Cie., Lausanne, and the two volumes of *Esquisses rythmiques* for the pianoforte.

NOTE.—The preceding suggestions have been formulated with the idea of helping the teacher of Eurhythmics to find new exercises. The third part of Rhythmic Movement will contain a number of examples of new rhythmic combinations, carefully arranged and systematised.

SINGING.

Teachers can apply many of these rhythmic exercises to singing (*i.e.*, those of control, inhibition, counterpoint, phrasing, twice as fast and slow, etc.). In the exercises for dissociated movements, singing may be substituted for movements of the arms, legs, head, etc.

EURHYTHMICS AND PIANOFORTE TECHNIQUE.

The teacher of any instrument can apply all the exercises of the method to the technique of the arms or fingers. They can all be turned into technical exercises for a particular instrument; they form the "bridge" between the study of rhythm *per se* (rhythmic development of the whole organism) and the study of specialized rhythm for the pianoforte, violin, organ, etc., when only one part of the body is at work.

In the series of examples, collected at the end of this volume under the title of "Eurhythmics applied to Pianoforte Technique," it is shown how certain exercises can be used in practising five-finger exercises. They can be used in the same way in practising intervals and series of chords, whether played together or as arpeggi.

Teachers of the pianoforte will recognize that there are great possibilities in the application of these exercises to pianoforte technique; they accustom the fingers to the rapid alternation of rest and attack, and to dissociated movements of all kinds, those which concern nuances and dynamics, as well as those which concern unequal note-values and different kinds of touch.

EURHYTHMICS APPLIED TO PIANOFORTE TECHNIQUE.

Anyone who has studied Eurhythmics with perseverance for the necessary length of time will recognize that the instrumentalist—be he a performer on the pianoforte, violin, or wind-instrument—can and should profit from his studies not only in a purely musical sense but also from the point of view of instrumental technique.

Up to the present there has been no bridge between the teaching of Eurhythmics and that of instrumental technique. Very few pianoforte-teachers know our special exercises, which aim at harmonizing the physical and spiritual instincts, educating the powers of feeling, and rendering the whole organism rhythmical. And so they are not in a position to utilise the knowledge, possessed by the student of Eurhythmics, for the special studies which they have in hand. It is more than likely that sooner or later some virtuoso will write a book of instrumental technique based directly on the system, in which each of the exercises destined for the whole body will be applied to the movements of the hand and arm. Meanwhile we wish briefly to indicate how rhythmic exercises can be applied to pianoforte technique, and how this study may be closely allied to the general education which is the object of the method.

It is not our intention to give a complete exposition of this wide subject. For that, several volumes would be necessary. We wish simply to indicate some guiding threads which may help the student of Eurhythmics in his work of adaptation, and will allow of his applying his acquired experience to his work at the pianoforte.

It is of first importance that the economic principle upon which so much stress is laid in the method, *i.e.*, that every movement must be carried out with the minimum of muscular energy, should be applied to the technical study of the instrument.

It is of great advantage that, before going to the pianoforte, the pupil should be equipped with the muscular mechanism necessary to the study of the instrument, that the muscles of arm, hand, and fingers should be prepared, by means of contraction and relaxation exercises, for all combined and dissociated movements. After a certain period, he will localise these exercises on the pianoforte, and will continue them till he feels able to overcome all unnecessary muscular and nervous resistance. It is indeed this unconscious resistance which constitutes the principal obstacle to freedom in the pianist's movements.

Here are a few examples which, with a view to clearness, brevity, and simplicity, we limit to five-finger exercises:

and we beg the reader to adapt these exercises himself to other pianistic forms.

N.B.—Five-finger exercises can be practised in the following ways:

1.  etc.

or

 etc.

in all the major and minor keys.

2.  etc.

and so on through the whole cycle of major and minor scales.

3.  etc.

and so on, rising chromatically.

EXERCISES.

(A) EXERCISES IN DISSOCIATED OR COMBINED MOVEMENTS FOR THE WHOLE ARM, FOREARM, HAND, AND FINGERS. EXERCISES IN THE USE OF THE PEDAL.

(a) EXERCISES.

To be practised first with each hand separately, then with hands together.

(b) EXERCISE IN DISSOCIATED MOVEMENTS.

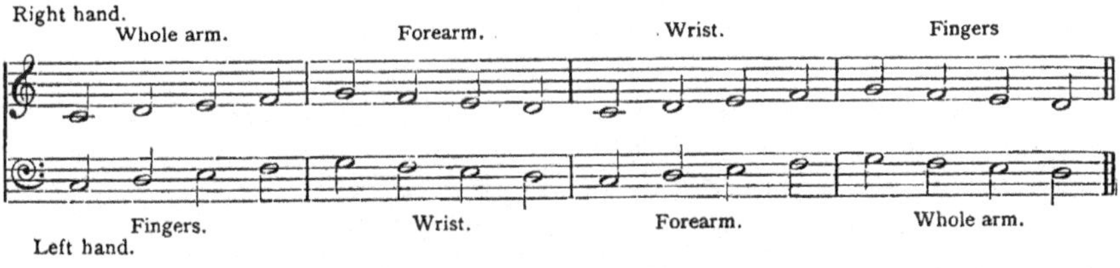

And so on with all possible combinations.

(c) DIFFERENT MOVEMENTS OF THE FINGERS.

Each hand separately, then both hands together.

* *See* Mlle. Blanche Selva, page 90.

Combined movements.

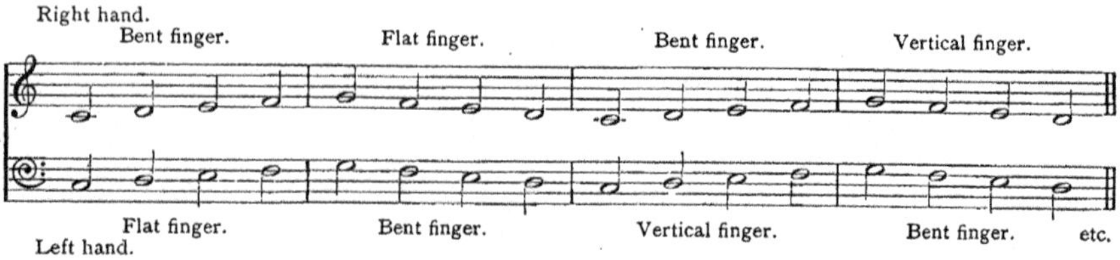

The same with combined movements of the hand, forearm, etc.

(*d*) THE WRIST IN LEGATO PLAYING.

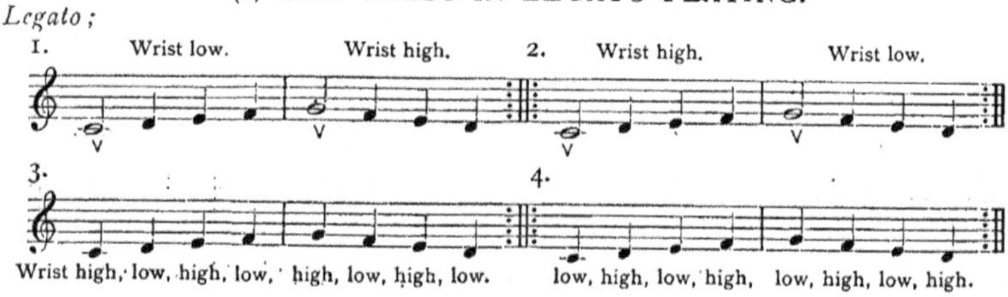

The same exercise, the pupil responding immediately to the command "raise" or "lower." To be played in different tempi.

Combined movements.

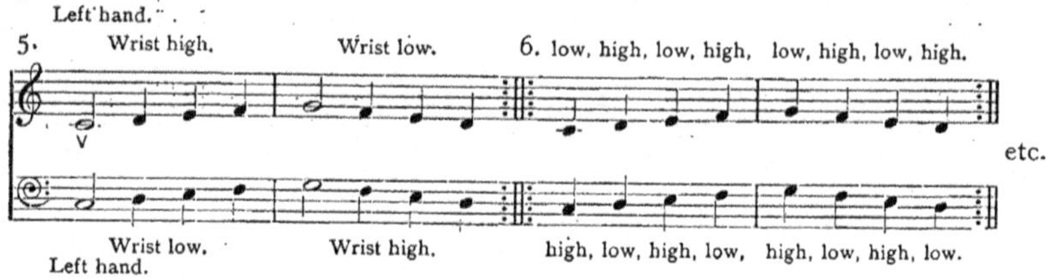

(*e*) COMBINATION OF VERTICAL AND HORIZONTAL MOVEMENTS.

3.
Left hand.
Right hand.
Left hand.
etc.
4.
etc.
8va...
loco
etc.
5.
6.
7.
etc.
8.
9a.
etc.

b.

At the command "left," the left hand plays *staccato*, the other hand continuing to play *legato*, or vice versâ.

(*f*) EXERCISES IN THE USE OF THE PEDAL.

Musicians who wish to write a complete treatise on this subject will do well to look out passages in classical works necessitating the use of the pedal, and to compose appropriate exercises on these models.

(1) Both hands together.

Pianoforte.

Pedal.

etc.

(2)

(3)

Pianoforte.

Pedal.

(4)

(5)

Pianoforte.

Organ.

The pupil must be careful to give each note its exact value.

(6) (7)

These and similar exercises can be turned into inhibition or incitation exercises.

(8)

To be practised with the rhythms suggested in 1 to 7; exercises on the use of the two pedals should be thought out and practised.

E.g.:

(*B*) THE APPLICATION OF THE SPECIAL METRIC AND RHYTHMIC EXERCISES TO PIANOFORTE TECHNIQUE.

All the preceding exercises have been concerned with technique in general. In the following we shall apply the principles of our method in a more detailed way. Recapitulating all the principal subjects dealt with in the two volumes of Rhythmic Movement, we shall give two or three examples of each, showing how they may be applied to the study of pianoforte technique, with a view to helping students of Eurhythmics in their instrumental studies and to showing them how they may benefit in these studies from their previous work.

(*a*) METRIC EXERCISES.

I. *Regular accents, equal beats.*

1. 

2. 

The same exercise, but beginning on D, E, F, G, etc.

3. 

And so on, accenting in turn every 5th, 6th, 7th, 8th, or 9th quaver.

To be practised in all keys and tempi, with scales, arpeggi, 3rds, 6ths, octaves, etc.

The same using different fingers.

4.  etc.

These can all be used as inhibition or incitation exercises, the pupil accenting a note, changing the place of the accent, or accentuating differently with each hand at the command *Hopp* given by the teacher.

E.g.:

5.  etc.

II. *Regular accents, unequal beats.*

I. 

2.

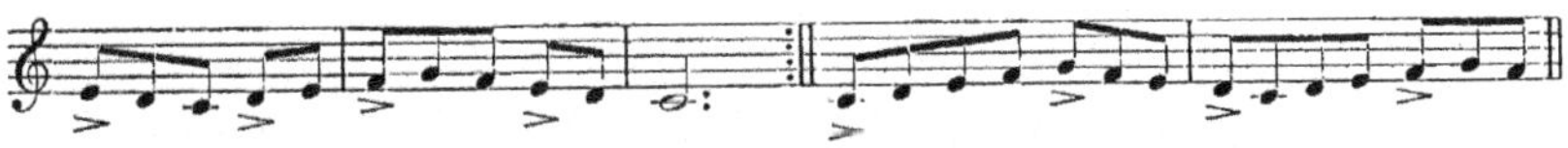

etc.

3.  etc.

4.  etc.

5. 6.

III. *Irregular accents; pathetic (i.e., expressive) accents.*

The pupil plays these exercises with regular accents on the beat (whether these are equal or unequal). At *Hopp* he accentuates the quaver following.

1. 

etc.

The same, but the right hand gives the accent on the first quaver after *Hopp*, the left hand on the second quaver.

2. 

etc.

To be combined with the preceding exercises.

All the preceding exercises are now to be practised with different note-values and rhythmic formulas, instead of only with equal notes.

E.g.:  The same with: 

(b) DYNAMICS.

To be varied and combined in different ways, as in the preceding exercises.

(c) AGOGICS.

I. *Accelerando and ritardando treated mathematically.*

The same exercise, changing triplets into quadruplets, quadruplets into quintuplets, etc.

II. *Accelerando and ritardando to be practised according to a given scheme.*

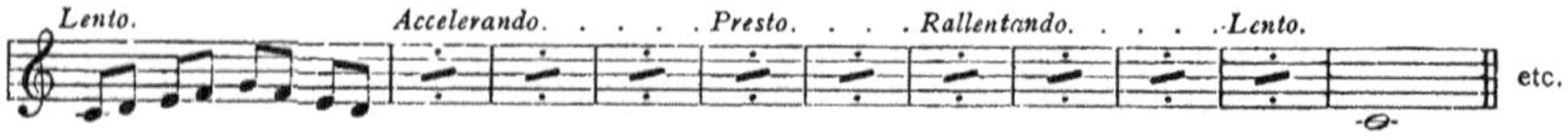

(*d*) THE ANACRUSIS AND PHRASING.

Different phrasing with each hand.

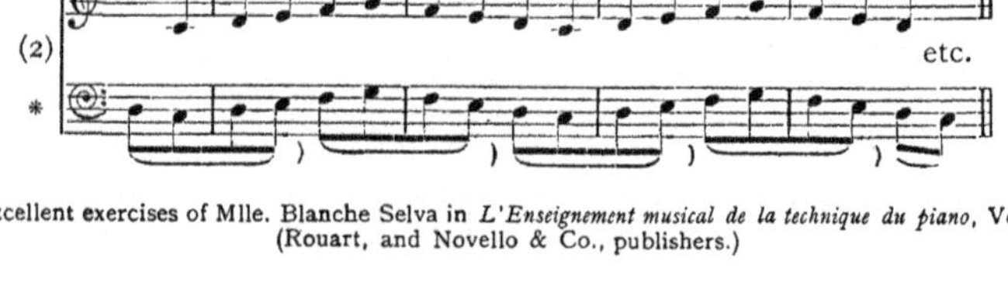

* *Cf.* the excellent exercises of Mlle. Blanche Selva in *L'Enseignement musical de la technique du piano*, Vol. I. and II. (Rouart, and Novello & Co., publishers.)

(3)

(*e*) BREATHING AND RESTS.

The same used as an inhibition exercise.

The same singing, and at *Hopp* continuing to sing in imagination during the rests.

The same with a prearranged rhythm.

The same with both hands:

* The pupil must continue singing in imagination.

Rhythmic themes containing rests:

(1) (2)

(*f*) SYNCOPATION.

The same as an incitation exercise (*i.e.*, syncopating at *Hopp*).

(*g*) TWO AND THREE TIMES AS FAST AND SLOW.

Incitation exercises.

To be combined with all the preceding exercises.

(*h*) RHYTHMIC COUNTERPOINT.

Counterpoint in half-values.

(5)

(*i*) POLYRHYTHM—CANON—TWO AGAINST THREE, ETC.

I. *Polyrhythm.*

(1)

(2)

(3)

II. *Canon.*

(4)

(5)

(6)

etc.

III. *Two against three, etc.*

The sign : increases each note by one quarter of its original value.

IV. *Two against three, ete., with one hand.*

It is clear that the suggested exercises are lacking in all harmonic and æsthetic value and in a more complete method, should be revised and rendered more musical.

By substituting the scale, chords, or appeggi for the five-finger exercise, an infinite variety of new exercises can be obtained.

It is to be hoped that these brief suggestions may incite specialists to create new types of technical exercises applicable to their particular instruments.

etc.
4
5
6
7
8
9
10
11

12
13
14
15
16

7
8
9

47

4

5

6

7

10

11

Two Groups or two Soloists.

14 

Groups and Solois

15

Two Soloists or two Groups.

18

19

23

Each phrase-fragment to be interpreted by a Group or a Soloist.

24

25

Groups and Soloists.

26

Groups and Soloists.

CPSIA information can be obtained
at www.ICGtesting.com
Printed in the USA
BVOW09s0101051217
501912BV00017B/927/P

9 780282 360412